IRISH HORSE-RACING
An Illustrated History

Irish

JOHN WELCOME

Horse-racing

AN ILLUSTRATED HISTORY

Gill and Macmillan

First published 1982 by
Gill and Macmillan Ltd
with associated companies in
London, New York, Delhi, Hong Kong,
Johannesburg, Lagos, Melbourne,
Singapore, Tokyo

© John Welcome 1982

7171 1046 X

Origination by Healyset, Dublin
Printed in the Republic of Ireland by
Criterion Press Ltd, Dublin

Contents

Sources of Illustrations

The authors and publishers wish to thank the following for permission to reproduce illustrations. Numbers refer to the pages on which the illustrations appear; (b), (c) and (t) following a page reference indicates that the illustration in question is positioned at the bottom, the centre, or the top of the page, respectively.

J. Cashman Jnr, Dublin 142, 163
G.A. Duncan, Dublin 124, 174, 194, 204, 205, 207
Fox Photos, London 173
Frank Griggs 108(b)
Illustrated London News 122(b) (c) (t)
Independent Newspapers Ltd, Dublin 190, 198, 199, 211
Irish Georgian Society 12
Irish Press, Dublin 146
Irish Times, Dublin 152, 166, 171, 181
Thomas Lethbridge, Pittrodrie House Gallery, Pitcaple, Aberdeenshire 48–9, 50–51
Marquis of Waterford 36(b) (t), 37, 39
W.W. Rouch, Marlborough, Wiltshire 150
Sport and General, London 93, 102, 130, 136, 147, 178, 203, 209
The Times, London 143

Every effort has been made to contact copyright holders, but if any have been inadvertently overlooked, the publishers will be pleased to make the necessary arrangements at the first opportunity.

Acknowledgments

I wish to express my thanks to all who have given me their assistance in the compilation of this book. Special mention must be made of the following for the trouble to which they went in helping me: Lord Killanin and Captain Luke Mullins for the history of Galway; Mr Nesbit Waddington and Mr Joseph Collins for Bellewstown and Laytown; Lieutenant-General P. A. Mulcahy and Mr Tommy Murphy for Baldoyle; Mr Andrew Moore for Punchestown; Mr Louis Noonan for Navan and Mr Max Fleming for Tramore. Virginia Dessain of *The European Racehorse* generously gave of her time in helping to trace photographs as did David Watkinson of *Owners*, and I must also thank John Ironside of Wexford for his invaluable photographic skill where reproductions were required.

I owe a particular debt of gratitude to the Marquis of Waterford who not only made available to me the pictures from his family collection of the the third Marquis and his exploits, but also gave me a copy of the privately printed memoir and hunting diary of that great administrator. Finally I must thank Mr Colm Croker for his meticulous reading of the script which has rescued my carelessness from many errors.

If I have omitted anyone I can only apologise. I must also make clear that responsibility for any statements of opinion, errors, omissions, or mistakes is mine alone. In a short survey such as this it is impossible to cover everything. I have tried to concentrate on the highlights and perhaps I may ask the reader, in the words of John Jorrocks when advising an ingenuous youth on buying a horse:

> Be to his faults a little blind,
> Be to his virtues ever kind

if, indeed, virtues there are.

J.W.

I

Brehon Laws and Early Days

1

The racing of horses in Ireland is as old as the nation itself. In the pre-Christian era the Red Branch Knights raced amongst themselves, matching their horses against each other, as did the Fianna warrior corps in the third century A.D. The racecourse then was often the king's or chief's own exercise green, and laws were laid down defining how far he was liable in case of injury to horse or rider. If such injury was the result of an accidental fall or interference by another competitor, then the chief was held blameless, but if it came about from badly maintained ground or 'chasms' on the course, then he incurred a heavy fine, the severity of which depended upon the extent of his negligence. Whether the fine ever found its way to the injured party by way of compensation is not revealed.

Horse-racing, however, was not confined to such private and aristocratic occasions. It took place also at the public assemblies or fairs, whose origins went back to pagan times. These fairs were held for the purpose of transacting all sorts of business — marriages were celebrated, deaths recorded, laws debated and defined, methods of defence agreed; but always they were followed by sports and games, and of these sports and games the most popular was horse-racing. In fact one of the derivations ascribed to the word *oenach* (fair) is 'a contention of horses'. And so important was horse-racing in the mythology of the people that in an old fable, *The Voyage of Bran*, one of the delights of heaven was said to be the racing of horses 'over a glorious sweep of country'.

As time went on the Brehon Laws laid down regulations for the upkeep and maintenance of public fair-greens, which had to be cleared and kept free of undergrowth, trees and other obstructions so that racing could take place upon them, and those who were made responsible for this work incurred considerable fines if it was inadequately carried out.

The most famous of these fairs was held at 'the Curragh of the

1

maccerpil

Liffey' or, as we know it, the Curragh of Kildare. From earliest times some writers were already referring to it as 'the Curragh of the Races', and the Gaelic word *currech* was used by them as a generic term for racecourse. The racing which took place there was presided over by the King of Leinster, or if he was not in residence at his palace of Dún Ailinn on the edge of the great plain, this honour was delegated to one of his princes.

The riders at the Curragh were scions of the upper classes, for the Brehon Laws decreed that 'none but a noble's son might ride in a race', and further laid down that horsemanship was required teaching for 'the sons of chiefs in fosterage' and that such instruction should start at an early age. Until a boy reached the age of seven his horse was to be provided by his father and after that age by his foster-father. Furthermore, foster-fathers had to find suitable mounts for their charges to ride in races. Sons of the *féine* (farmers), on the other hand, were not to be provided with horses, since no instruction in the art of riding was to be given them.

The horses contesting these races were frequently not home bred but were imported, those coming from Wales being especially valued. 'A steed and trappings brought from over the sea' was the tribute demanded by the King of Munster from the King of Uí Liatháin and duly received by him. The 'trappings' were in fact minimal, so far as

2

riding horses were concerned, those kept for chariot-driving being more elaborate. Saddles were not used at all at that time; the most that was done was to place a thick cloth or 'dillat' between the rider and his horse. This cloth was later developed into a rudimentary saddle (*diallait* is still the Irish word for 'saddle'), but even then stirrups were never used, and a 'steed-leap' or vault onto the horse's back was the method of mounting.

The bridle had a single rein attached to a nose-band; this came between the horse's ears, where it was held in place by a strap corresponding roughly to the present-day brow-band. It was of no assistance in guiding the horse, and for this purpose an *echlasc* (horse-rod) was provided for the rider. This was a stout stick made of yew or ash, and with it the rider indicated with varying degrees of severity the direction he wished his mount to take. Sometimes in races this rod, heavy and unwieldy though it was, was used as a sort of whip. Later, as bridles developed, this horse-rod lost its original usage and became 'an instrument for urging' or a goad with a metal point or a lash at its end. Finally it developed into the whip as we know it today.

Grotesque representation of a horseman, using a horse-rod, from the Book of Kells (seventh century).

3

Most of the horses kept for racing were stallions, the gelding or 'garraun' being looked down upon as a work-horse. The racehorses were fed on grass and corn; and when a race was in contemplation they were specially trained for it, though the methods employed to get them fit have unfortunately not come down to us.

2

Despite tribal wars, invasions and internecine strife, racing lived on in the lives of the people, especially at the Curragh. There are records of its taking place there amongst the Anglo-Normans, and a free translation from the Latin poem giving an account of it runs:

> Its name, from wearied steeds, the Curragh takes —
> A name of yore in tongue vernacular given,
> But which in Greek is called an Hippodrome —
> Because this plain on ev'ry side's cut up
> By the tired hoofs o' th' Geraldines, when there
> That martial race, exulting, exercise
> Their steeds, and try their mettle — thus to test
> Which fleetest is, ere ent'ring for the Stakes.

The horses, whether ridden by the Geraldines or not, continued to be imported. It appears that the ancestors of the most famous of the early breeds of Irish horse, the 'hobby', 'haubini' or 'urbino' came from Spain. These 'hobbies' were much the same type as the Scottish galloways, small animals standing not much more than 13 hands. Tough and hardy, they were, in the words of one chronicler, 'in racing wonderful swift, in gallop false and indifferent'. This, if it means anything, appears to indicate that their abilities overcame the deficiencies in their action. Judges of horseflesh, as always, found it hard to agree, for another wrote: 'Ireland produces nothing worthy of mention but corn and excellent horses, which the inhabitants term "urbinos".' They were raced successfully throughout the country, and when in Tudor times the first English royal stud was established at Tutbury in Staffordshire hobbies were imported from Ireland for breeding purposes — a practice which was by no means universally popular. 'Such outlandish horses as are daily brought over unto us', protested one angry commentator, '. . . such as the genet of Spain, the coercer of Naples, the hobbie of Ireland . . .' Nevertheless Gervase Markham, the first of the many pundits down the years to propound theories of breeding in print, could say of the hobbies, when comparing them with the 'barbs' or imports from Northern Africa: 'When the best Barbaries that ever were in my remembrance were in their prime, I saw them overunne by a black Hobbie at Salisburie.' But even after presenting such favourable evidence he went on to maintain that neither breed could match the stamina and speed of the 'plaine bredde' English horse.

In their native country, however, the racing of hobbies and other horses was still necessarily of a rudimentary nature owing to the lack of communications, for roads were only primitive tracks. Sometimes strands and beaches at low tide were used as racecourses. Racing at fairs persisted too — as indeed it was to do until well into the nineteenth century. If there was a centre and focal point for it all, it remained the Curragh. In April 1634 Lord Digby and the Earl of Ormond matched each other's horses there over four miles, and the great Earl of Cork in backing Lord Digby lost 'a new beaver hat to Mr Ferrers, one of the Lord Deputy's gentlemen'. About this time too racing began at Bellewstown, making it, along with the Curragh, one of the oldest courses in the country to stage meetings continually down to the present day.

Racing then usually took place on a Sunday, but Cromwell and puritanism put a stop to that. Indeed the puritans all but killed racing in the country. Holding it to be one of the devil's works, they made every effort to stamp it out, and such informal meetings as survived had to be carried on clandestinely and in conditions of secrecy.

A revival of sorts came with Charles II, who, although he closed down the Tutbury stud, encouraged the breeding and racing of horses. But long after Charles had established Newmarket as the headquarters of racing in England and set up some sort of organisation there together with a system for deciding disputes, racing at the Curragh continued to be an adjunct of the fair, uncontrolled and always liable to provoke outbursts of violence. There was, it is true, 'a race run yearly there in March or April for a plate of a hundred guineas which are advanced by the subscription of several gentlemen; and the course is four measured miles'. The 'several gentlemen' presumably made their own rules and enforced them as best they could. However, Sir William Temple, MP for Carlow and a diplomat in the service of Charles II, appreciating what had been done at Newmarket, endeavoured to bring about a similar situation at the Curragh. In a memorandum which he submitted to the Lord Lieutenant he proposed that 'two judges of the field' be appointed to sit as arbitrators to determine all disputes and — an interesting throwback to the days of the old Irish kings — made the further recommendation that the Lord Lieutenant himself should be present at all meetings in a supervisory capacity or, if he could not appear, should appoint a deputy to act on his behalf. Temple did succeed in obtaining from the royal coffers an annual grant of £100 for the purchase of a plate, known as the King's Plate, to be run for each year in September, each runner to carry 12st. But nothing came of his suggestions for control, and when the Earl of Clarendon, during his short and turbulent viceroyalty in the reign of James II, visited the Curragh in his private capacity to view the fair and the races he was appalled by the scenes of violence he witnessed. He was, however, greatly impressed by the racecourse itself, commenting that 'The common where the race is held is a much finer turf than Newmarket.'

3

The Revolution of 1688, the Battle of the Boyne and the Williamite campaign put an end for the time being to whatever hope there was of bringing organisation and control into Irish racing and breeding. That racing was in some measure carried on in the less disturbed parts of the country is undeniable, but no reliable records of it now exist. Nevertheless it is to this period that we owe the origins of steeplechasing. This sport sprang from the 'pounding matches' much favoured at the time by the sprigs of the nobility and gentry in Galway and the west. Owners who had sufficient confidence in their horses' powers of jumping and staying would, over the claret or elsewhere, make a match to test their mounts. A place and time would be arranged, and there the two rivals would take each other on across a country until one or the other either fell or was ridden into the ground. The loser was then held to have been 'pounded', a verb which passed into the vocabulary of the Regency bucks and their Victorian successors who sailed across High Leicestershire a generation later.

Gradually, as peace of a sort was restored to the shattered country, racing revived. 'Horse-racing is become a great diversion in the country', *Dickson's Dublin Intelligence* recorded in 1731, going on to instance a case where the threat to the commons of a town that they would be taken up for some public use was frustrated by the townspeople 'continuing to employ them to a greater advantage by making a horse-course around them'. And a record exists of a race for 'a Fourty Pound Plate given by ye Gentlemen of ye County of Gallway, run for on ye course of Park ye 19th September 1741'.

The penal laws which made it an offence for any Catholic to own or keep in his possession any horse, gelding or mare to the value of £5 or more were largely frustrated or disregarded by the sporting fraternity. For although these laws stipulated that 'If any person of the Protestant religion shall make a discovery thereof on oath to any two justices of the peace, he can, on paying £5, appropriate such horse to himself,' instances were rife of racing men conspiring together to defeat those who attempted to take advantage of this provision. In one well-published incident 'A Catholic who owned one of the most celebrated racers in Ireland worth 200 guineas, being informed that a person was about to seize him and pay the price fixed by law, mounted the horse and presented him to a Protestant friend.'

These irregularities were frowned on by the authorities, and it was thought that the all but universal habit of making matches contributed to them. Accordingly an act was passed in 1739 prohibiting matches and making it illegal to run for any plate of less than £120 in value. But, again, this act was largely ignored, and little attempt was made to enforce it. Nevertheless it was appreciated by those who cared for the well-being of the sport that some effort should be made to exercise control over it and to keep a record of races and results. Here they looked towards England to ascertain what progress was being made there in these matters.

As far back as 1679 a Mr John Nelson of Newmarket had kept a register of horse matches, but it was not until 1741 that John Cheney, who had commenced his own register in 1727, recorded an Irish race. Appropriately enough, this was run at the Curragh and was won by Lord Bessborough's Almazer. Cheney died in 1751, but his register was carried on in the following year by Reginald Heber, who addressed his 'grateful Devoirs' not only to 'most noble and worthy Patrons of England and Wales' but also to 'the Gentlemen of Ireland', thus for the first time giving semi-official cognisance to a record of Irish racing.

4

It was in the year 1752 that there took place the famous match between Mr Edmund Blake and Mr O'Callaghan from Buttevant Church in Co. Cork to the spire of St Leger Church, four and a half miles over a natural country. This occurrence, it is generally agreed, eventually led to the addition of a new word to the English language, for from this contest and from the earlier 'pounding matches' all 'steeplechasing' derives.

Important developments were also taking place on the more orthodox racecourses. A few years before the Buttevant race there occurred two interconnected events which caused sensations in the Irish racing world — and indeed outside it — and which may well have hastened the desire for control and the accurate recording of races, distances and weights.

A Mr Archbold owned a grey mare called Irish Lass who had gained fame for her speed and staying power and who had won the Royal Plate at the Curragh in 1745 and 1747. A serving soldier, Sir Ralph Gore, had brought with him to Ireland a horse which he had raced successfully in England under the name of Othello. For reasons best known to himself, once the horse had crossed the Irish Sea Sir Ralph renamed him Black and All Black and almost

Black and All Black.

Bajazet.

immediately matched him against Irish Lass. The match attracted great attention, with the nobility and gentry backing Black and All Black and the lower orders laying their money on Irish Lass. The weight of the money, as may be imagined, was for Black and All Black, and he was accordingly installed as a firm favourite.

Mr Archbold, however, in order to improve his mare's chances, attached a *paidrín* (Irish for 'rosary') to her neck before he sent her out to carry not only his money but his prayers. Whether it was the result of heavenly intervention or not, Irish Lass defeated the invader and came home to an almost hysterical welcome from the crowd.

She thereupon became a national heroine and was universally known as 'the Paddereen Mare'. So far did the fame of her prowess extend that she was actually excluded by name in the articles for certain races. At Kilcoole, for instance, the following race was advertised: 'A purse of £20 by any horse, mare or gelding carrying 10st, winners of last week's April Plate at the Curragh and the grey mare, now called Mr Archbold's mare, only excepted.' The article further went on to say (and this may have struck an ominous note in the minds of those desiring better control of the sport): 'Every horse to run four rounds, no crossing or jostling, but the last half-mile of each heat, and that by the two foremost only.'

Black and All Black, however, was made the subject of no such restrictions, and in 1751, anxious to restore his horse's reputation, Gore matched him against the Earl of March's Bajazet for the sum of 1,000 guineas, a very considerable stake in those days. Black and All Black was to carry 10st, Bajazet 10st 7lb.

Lord March, then a young man, was later to become the last Duke of Queensberry, the infamous 'Old Q', the 'Rake of Piccadilly'. Even at this early date his reputation was far from unsullied, and he was well known for sharp practice on the racecourse. 'He loves betting, he loves eating, he loves money, he loves women,' Thackeray said of him. Although he was himself a useful amateur rider, he preferred on this occasion to put up a professional. The jockey could not make the required weight, so Lord March had a 'shotted belt' made for him. This was of leather with pouches sewn into it to receive a number of lead weights, and the jockey was to buckle it around his waist before weighing out. It is as certain as anything can be that March instructed the jockey to jettison the belt before or during the riding of the race and to recover it as he came to weigh in. In any event, that is just what the jockey did, though it availed him little, for Black and All Black won easily.

A Prospect of the great Match Run on the Curragh Sept.ʳ 5.ᵗʰ 1751 for 1000 Guineas Between Black & all Black Belonging to the Honᵇˡᵉ Sʳ Ralph Gore & Bajazet the Property of the Rᵗ Honᵇˡᵉ the Earl of March won wᵗʰ Ease by the former.

Well aware of March's reputation and suspecting some roguery, Sir Ralph Gore had a close watch kept on his opponent's rider. As he returned to the scale Gore saw the belt being handed back to him. Instantly he had both jockey and his accomplice brought before him and accused of the offence. The terrified jockey immediately implicated his master. A challenge followed, and March was called out to face the consequences of his actions on the field of honour.

Not only had March a bad reputation for trickery, but he was also noted for not caring very much for facing powder and shot. Armed with this knowledge, Sir Ralph Gore, who appears to have possessed a macabre sense of humour, laid his preparations accordingly. When he arrived on the duelling field he was accompanied by several servants who bore with them an elaborate and highly polished oak coffin. On its lid was March's coat of arms, his name, the date of his birth, and also the date of his death, being that of the very day upon which the two duellists were facing each other. When March enquired the reason for this charade Gore ordered the servants to carry the coffin over and lay it at his opponent's feet. As he read the inscription March blanched. His fears were in no way allayed when Gore, bowing courteously to him, made the following speech: 'My dear fellow, you are, of course, aware that I never miss my man, and as I feel myself in excellent form this morning I have not a shadow of doubt upon my mind but this oaken box will shortly be better calculated for you than your present dress.'

That decided the noble earl. Hastily he made a complete admission of guilt and the most humble apology. These were accepted with silent scorn, Gore turning on his heel and leaving the field and the coffin to his disgraced opponent. The story quickly got about, and as a result March was cut in some of his clubs, there being even talk of expelling him from White's. Six years later, however, he was elected one of the early members of the Jockey Club. Ironically, almost his first action there was to initiate and then sign a memorandum stressing the importance of jockeys carrying the correct weight and laying down severe penalties for their failure to do so.

Although the Earl of March was scarcely the most appropriate person to voice this complaint and issue this warning, abuses such as weight-switching and other trickery were becoming more and more widespread, and it was evident to those in the sport who were both honourable and responsible that something should be done to check them.

2

The Turf Club
and the growth of Steeplechasing

1

The year 1750 is now generally accepted as the date on which the Jockey Club came into existence in England. At its inception it was more a social club where aristocratic owners could forgather to exchange opinions about the sport and its conduct rather than a governing body exercising and enforcing overall control. Its members, however, were accustomed to the exercise of privilege and power, and by a natural process authority accrued to them. It was not long before they became recognised as the controlling body in England for the governance of the sport.

Although no such body existed in Ireland and was not to appear for many years, the King's Plates, at least, were now made subject to a set of articles published in Dublin. It has to be said, however, that these articles were very loosely interpreted, for nobody had the power to enforce their sanctions. Indeed the clause concerning the settling of disputes was so vague as almost to invite controversy and litigation; as a classic example of ambiguity this rule is worth quoting in full:

> The Chief Governor or Governors (if present) are to appoint a Judge or Judges, to see the riders weighted, at the end of each heat, and to set down the place in which each horse, mare or gelding comes, and to decide any difference that shall arise; and in their absence the persons who are the owners of such horse, mare or gelding, may choose each a Judge before starting for those ends, unless the Governor shall appoint a deputy to do it in his absence.

It has been conjectured that when the Jockey Club assumed authority in England disputes from Ireland were referred to it in the absence of any governing body in the latter country. Certainly there is a record of this happening as early as 1757, when a case was

One of Thomas Conolly's racehorses, name unknown.

'sent on' (to use the modern expression) to the Jockey Club from the Curragh. This 'sending on' was probably at the instigation of Thomas Conolly, a great-nephew of Speaker Conolly, who had built the vast Palladian mansion at Castletown. Thomas Conolly was more sportsman than politician. He hunted his own hounds, earned the sobriquet of 'Squire' and was one of the early members of the Jockey Club, being the first of his countrymen to be so honoured. According to one of the historians of the club, 'He was at the very head of the Irish Turf of his day, winning Royal Plates beyond ordinary powers of calculation.'

For the most part, however, gentlemen appear to have settled their disputes amongst themselves as best they could or, when all other methods failed, had recourse either to litigation or to the time-honoured Irish decider, the duelling pistol. Nevertheless order of a sort was beginning to arrive. Cheney's *Calendar* was now listing local meetings in Ulster, Limerick, Meath and Galway. In the year 1750 which saw the founding of the Jockey Club no less than seventy-one meetings were advertised to take place in Ireland.

These listed meetings were, of course, far from being the only

12

ones to take place; they were merely those of which Cheney and later Heber took cognisance or those for which publicity and the registration of results were sought by their organisers. Many other matches and meetings of which no record now exists were still being run all over the country at fairs or other venues — gentlemen's parks and the like.

The Curragh, however, was by this time well established as the Irish Newmarket and the headquarters of the country's racing. Permanent stables had been built, and at least some sort of a stand or building to accommodate the owners and gentry so that they could have a reasonable view of the running of their horses. Sir Jonah Barrington has recorded that at about this time, when he and his brother were making a journey to Dublin, 'We passed over the famous raceground of the Curragh in good style; but as my brother had not given his horse time to lie down gently and rest himself in the ordinary way, the animal had no choice but to perform the feat of lying down when in full gallop — which he did very expertly just at the Curragh stand-house.'

At length, in 1790, almost certainly owing to the efforts of Thomas Conolly, an Irish governing body was founded. It was to be called the Turf Club to differentiate it from the Jockey Club. Once formed, it immediately gave its imprimatur to a publication by a Mr Pat Sharkey to be called the *Irish Racing Calendar*. This calendar, when published, set out the rules for election to the club or admission to the coffee-room at Kildare where its meetings were to take place, in much the same way as the English rules governed admission to the coffee-room at Newmarket, which later became the Jockey Club headquarters: 'His name to be put over the chimney the day before he is balloted for; there must be twelve members present, three black balls to exclude.' The rules also laid down that three members were to be elected Stewards, one to retire each year, the new Steward to be nominated by the retiring Steward 'subject to the approval of the members' — a system, incidentally, which, hallowed by tradition, remained in existence until recently swept away by the wind of modernisation and change.

The Rules and Orders of the Turf Club corresponded closely with those laid down by the Jockey Club and appear to owe their origin to Thomas Conolly's intimate knowledge and experience of the inner workings of the sister club. The first list of members was headed by His Grace the Duke of Leinster, the premier Irish peer, and contained, amongst those prominent in the ranks of nobility and gentry, the Hon. Arthur Wellesley, the future Duke of Wellington, and Sir John Carden, ancestor of the oppressive landlord in Parnell's time so frequently shot at by the tenantry as to earn for himself the name of 'Woodcock' Carden.

In Sharkey's first calendar eighteen courses coming under the jurisdiction of the Turf Club were named. Each of these courses except the Curragh was allocated one meeting in the year. The Curragh had two meetings in April and one each in the months of June, September and October. Ulstermen, true to their own independent tradition, maintained their own headquarters at the Maze, where the first races had taken place as early as 1640. Later the Prince of Orange, when staying with the Marquis of Downshire at Hillsborough, ordered the Collector of Customs in Belfast to donate an annual sum of £100 for the purpose of endowing a King's Cup. By a special dispensation of the Jockey Club, and as a sop to the religious susceptibilities of those responsible for racing in Ulster, stewards were permitted to insist that the starter on all their courses should carry a Bible, upon which, in the case of a false start, he was required to swear that he had not given 'the off'.

Improbable though this may sound, in the south, at Tralee, the articles of a race for a plate donated by 'the Gentlemen of the Profession of the Law in the County of Kerry' had an even more bizarre provision. The owner of each entry was required to have expended at least £200 in 'adverse litigation', those who had spent £1,000 and upwards in the same cause being given a weight allowance of 3lb. These conditions were drawn up and settled by none other than Daniel O'Connell in his seventh year at the Bar. The race was run on 29 August 1805 and was won by a Protestant clergyman, Rev. Mr Denis of Wicklow! The exact meaning of the words 'adverse litigation' was, to say the least, difficult to define, and, as might have been expected, the result of the race led to a dispute. This was only settled by the intervention of the Stewards of the Turf Club, who were gradually assuming wider authority and greater powers.

2

The rebellion of 1798 suspended all racing, but, considering the nature of the insurrection and the distressed state of the country, the suspension lasted for a surprisingly short time. Charles James Apperley, who as 'Nimrod' was later to become the first racing correspondent to be read all over the then English-speaking world, served during the rebellion with Sir Watkin Williams Wynn's Ancient British Fencibles or Light Dragoons, a regiment which earned for itself the soubriquet of the 'Bloody British' from the insurgents. Violent though they might have been in their methods of suppression, the 'Bloody British' did not neglect their sport, and Nimrod records that amongst the officers were three who had been Masters of Foxhounds and one who was shortly to take over a pack. In the intervals of campaigning, he says, 'a little racing was now and then picked up, an excellent private course being at hand'. Stationed at Athy, Co. Kildare, they were, moreover, well placed for the Curragh, and Nimrod notes that after the stables had been cleared of the rebels racing was resumed there. In fact it started again in the September of '98, and Nimrod immediately took advantage of it. Although he had been unsuccessful in private regimental racing, he always had an unerring eye for horseflesh, and this enabled him to pick up for 25 guineas a four-year-old colt by Belisarius which all his brother officers had crabbed for his action. On this colt at the Curragh he won six 'sweepstakes and matches' from six starts, the owner-rider being spurred on by the encouragements of Murphy, his Irish groom, lately in the service of the Duke of Leinster. 'Hould him hard, me jewel,' Murphy would roar as they entered the straight, 'and its all Dublin to a tatur garden!'

Nimrod also recorded that the poisoning, doping or otherwise criminally interfering with fancied horses which was prevalent in England at that time had not yet spread to Irish racing. On bringing one of his horses to the Curragh overnight he was shocked to find that a stable containing seven or eight of the following day's runners was unlocked and unguarded. Enquiring from a boy as to where the groom in charge was to be found, he received the answer 'Sure my master's in bed and he's drunk.' Nevertheless no harm came to any of the horses, which would not have been the case, Nimrod thought, in England in a similar situation. It was not, in fact, as Nimrod also records, until the hanging in 1812 of Dan Dawson, the head of the worst of the poisoning gangs, that this menace to the sport in England was swept away.

For much of his hunting, racing and writing career Nimrod frowned on steeplechasing as a bastard offshoot of the flat and as being unnecessarily dangerous to men or, more importantly, their horses. This attitude was shared by many if not most of the influential racing men of the day. Nevertheless the word 'steeplechasing' was maintaining its place in the language as a substitute for the alternative form 'steeplehunting' often previously used. In 1803 what has been recorded as 'the first regular steeplechase' was run in Ireland. It arose from a conversation at a hunt dinner and was almost certainly inspired by the tradition of the old 'pounding matches'. Although the result has not survived, a draft of the proposed conditions discloses that it was 'a sweepstake with added money of a hogshead of claret, a pipe of port and a quarter-cask of rum'. And in 1807 the *Irish Racing Calendar* employed the word 'steeplechase' for the first time to describe a match across country of six miles between Mr White's Terrara and Mr Weir's Comet.

Naturally enough, it was the fox-hunting fraternity who nurtured and developed this branch of the sport, the mounts in almost all

'The first red coat steeplechase.' Note the primitive 'stand house' in the background, the 'followers' mounted and unmounted and the family group by the single flag.

cases being their hunters. It was therefore agreed amongst them and decreed that unless the owner entered the horse himself, an affidavit had to be sworn by the person making the entry affirming, amongst other things, that the horse 'never started for match or Plate (but a fair hunter Plate), and has been actually used as a hunter, at the last season, and not only to get the name, but really as a hunter; nor has he been in sweats with the intention to run, but only from Lady Day last'.

Steeplechasing continued to gain in popularity, but at this time and for many years to come there were, of course, no 'enclosed' steeplechase tracks with made fences. The races continued to be run over a natural country from point to point, with instructions, often of the vaguest sort, being given to the riders as to the course they should take. On some occasions men with flags were placed in ditches dotted about the line to be followed. By holding up the flags when they saw that the order to start had been given they provided a rudimentary guide for the riders.

An English visitor returning from a hunting and sporting holiday

16

in Ireland referred to the popularity and prevalence of steeplechasing there, describing it as 'a sort of racing for which the Paddies are particularly famous, and in which, unless the rider has pluck and his prad goodness, they cannot expect to get well home'. The latter part of this sentence was all too true, for in a race at Lismore about this time the winner fell four times and the third horse six times. 'In all twelve falls, but nobody killed. Betting: evens at starting that there would be six falls.'

The obstacles were fearsome indeed. One writer told a friend that he had seen two Irish horses in a race leap a river which measured twenty-two feet clear. On St Patrick's Day 1813 a race took place at Rathangan, Co. Roscommon, over a distance of six miles; among the obstacles which the entrants were required to clear were 'six walls five feet high and several yawning ditches'.

It is not perhaps surprising that another returning English visitor wrote in some astonishment: 'This system of horsemanship, dangerous in the extreme, has become the favourite amusement of the young fox-hunters of the day,' while the author of *The History and Delineation of the Horse*, published in 1809, recorded that 'The Irish [horses] are the highest and the steadiest leapers in the world.'

Crossing a road in an early steeplechase over natural country. Note spectator holding a direction flag in the background.

3

Royalty, Birdcatcher and Harkaway

1

By the beginning of the nineteenth century Irish racing was emerging
from its early or chrysalis period. The first handicap to be run at the
Curragh had taken place in 1787, being won by Mr F. Savage's
Governor. In the early years of the new century the practice of
holding mains of cocking at gentlemen's houses before racing (Mr
Bowes Daly's lawn at Athgarvan Lodge was a particularly favoured
spot on the days before Curragh meetings) was dying out, and it had
been abandoned altogether in 1819, when 'The Rules for Matching
and Fighting Cocks in Ireland' were dropped from the *Racing
Calendar*. In 1817 an attempt was made to emulate the Epsom Oaks
by the institution of the Irish Oaks Stakes at the Curragh, but this
was a failure. The old-style matches too were becoming fewer and
fewer and were being replaced by Corinthian races between gentlemen. The first of these to be run at the Curragh in 1822 was won
by the Marquis of Clanricarde on his own horse Penguin.

An enormous fillip was given to the whole racing scene by the
visit to the Curragh in 1821 of the reigning monarch, George IV. A
racing man himself, the King had won the Derby in 1788 with
his horse Sir Thomas, and countless other races with horses owned
by him. He had stood loyally by his jockey Sam Chifney in the
famous row with the Jockey Club over the running of Escape at
Newmarket. He was also a good judge of a horse and in his younger
days had been a bold and skilful rider. Now at sixty, ill, dissipated
and debauched and still suffering from the effects of a recent
operation, he nevertheless had not lost his love of the Turf, and when
the Stewards of the Turf Club invited him to a special meeting to be
held in his honour at the Curragh on 1 September he eagerly
accepted. Before the day arrived he was, however, afflicted by what
Creevy, the gossip and diarist, quoting from a correspondent,
described as an attack of 'wherry-go-nimbles'. The resulting diarrhoea

did not abate, and intelligence of the King's condition was conveyed to the stewards. They immediately realised that something must be done to provide a convenience for the royal person. A special stand and a banqueting room had already been erected, but now the Duke of Leinster, who was the King's godson, was given the task of supervising the additional work of building a suitable 'retiring house'. He posted to Dublin and returned bringing with him a specialist in such matters who supervised the construction.

It was as well that these precautions had been taken, for during the first race the King was 'compelled to bolt' and, according to some accounts, later complained that the seat was too small for the comfortable accommodation of his ample proportions. If so, he soon recovered his good humour, for before leaving he presented the Duke of Leinster with a gold whip to be run for every year at the Curragh, along with the endowment of an annual sum of 100 guineas to be awarded with the whip. This was the precursor of the Royal Whip, still run at the Curragh.

Possibly owing to the cachet conferred upon it by the royal visit, racing in Ireland now began to thrive and prosper, although the year 1824 saw the discontinuance of the O'Darby Stakes at the Curragh, a race instituted in 1817 by the Stewards of the Turf Club in the hope that it would rank in importance with the English Derby. Their hopes were disappointed, for the race failed to attract the attention of the public or entries from owners and, as a result, had to be abandoned after only eight years. But in spite of this initial setback, the quality of racing was improving and the sport was entering an exciting new era of progress. This progress was exemplified during the next two decades in the careers of two of the greatest horses to appear in the history of the Irish Turf — Birdcatcher and Harkaway.

2

Before dealing with these two outstanding horses it is necessary to touch on the career of their immediate predecessor, the colt claimed to be the first Irish horse to hold his own in English classic company. This was Bran, bred by the Marquis of Sligo in 1831, two years before Birdcatcher was foaled. Bran was by Humphrey Clinker; as a two-year-old he showed high promise, and in the following year he was sent by Lord Sligo to England to take on the best. At York he won the Spring St Leger when ridden by Pat Connolly, one of the first Irish jockeys to cross the water and make a name for himself in England.

Bran was not entered for the 1834 Derby, which was won by Mr Batson's Plenipotentiary, ridden by Connolly. He won again, however, at the York August Meeting and was then sent to

Doncaster for the St Leger. Connolly was claimed for 'Plenipo', as he was universally known, and the mount on Bran was given to Sam Darling, the founding father of the Darling dynasty, who had won the race the year before on Rockingham. Bran ran a gallant race, finishing second two lengths behind Touchstone, who started at 50 to 1. 'Plenipo', who started a hot favourite, was never seen with a chance. All sorts of accusations were hurled about after the race, most of them at the unfortunate Mr Batson; it was even alleged that he had stopped his own horse by doping him with poison. It is most unlikely that anything of the sort happened. Apart from the fact that Touchstone was a very useful colt who started at a false price and later proved a successful sire, it was afterwards discovered that 'Plenipo', when being walked to the course as was the custom in those days, had slipped and fallen in the main street of Saffron Walden and damaged himself internally.

Two days after the St Leger Bran won the Gascoigne Stakes, easily beating Shillelagh, who had started second favourite for the St Leger and had been second to 'Plenipo' in the Derby. In the following year, 1835, he was second in the Ascot Gold Cup to Glencoe, who had won the previous year's Two Thousand Guineas and been third in the Derby, having the Oaks winner, Pussy, well behind him. Altogether he was not a bad torchbearer for his mighty successors.

3

The story of Birdcatcher's begetting is, as so often seems to be the case with great horses, especially in this period, a romantic one. Mr Bowes Daly of the Athgarvan Stud bred a colt, Bob Booty, who, although he did not run until he was four (which was by no means unusual then), quickly showed his worth by winning a King's Plate at the Curragh on his first appearance on a racecourse. Mr Daly then took him to England and won with him there. He was soon back in Ireland, however, and won another King's Plate and the Kildare Stakes, both at the Curragh. He was then retired to stud, where he proved a prolific sire of winners and dams of winners.

Mr Martin Joseph Blake, MP for Galway, one of the founding fathers of steeplechasing and known colloquially as 'the man for Galway', had a mare, Flight, by Irish Escape, whom he sent to Bob Booty. The result of this mating was a filly whom he called Guiccioli. A small and insignificant-looking chestnut, Guiccioli was better than she looked, for she won ten races for Mr Blake. Thinking little of her as a stud prospect when her racing career was over, Mr Blake sold her to Mr J. R. Hunter. Mr Hunter had been appointed first Keeper of the Match Book to the Irish Turf

Club in 1817, but this did not interfere with his activities in breeding and racing his own horses. He put Guiccioli to his stallion, Roller, who got her in foal. He was not, however, impressed with the likelihood of her producing anything of worth, and at a race meeting in Kilkenny he offered her, carrying her foal, to anyone who would give him £30 for her. A Mr John H. Jones was about to buy her when a friend put him off, saying: 'Why do you want to buy such a cut of a thing? She'll never breed hunters for you.' Subsequently she passed into the ownership of a Mr Knox of Brownstown House, the Curragh.

Mr Knox put Guiccioli, then aged eight, to Sir Hercules, a black horse who had been third in the St Leger and who was said to have been named after Sir Hercules Langrishe of Knocktopher Abbey. *Birdcatcher.*

Sir Hercules was owned by Lord Langford and stood at his stud at Summerhill, Co. Meath, at a fee of £10. The resulting foal was none other than Birdcatcher. But Mr Knox was fortunate in obtaining Sir Hercules's services, for the stallion was put up for auction at Doncaster in 1833, the year Birdcatcher was foaled, along with the rest of Lord Langford's bloodstock. He was sold for export to America, but for some reason the sale fell through. He lived on to the age of twenty-nine, siring many good winners amongst whom were Coronation, the winner of the 1841 Derby, and Leamington, the sire of Iroquois, the first American-bred horse ever to win the Derby. Guiccioli, it may be mentioned in passing, eight years later produced a full brother to Birdcatcher, Faugh-a-Ballagh, who, in winning the St Leger in 1844, became the first Irish-bred horse to win an English classic.

Shortly after his birth Birdcatcher contracted severe inflammation of the lungs, and it was thought that he could not survive. Thanks to the care of Mr Knox and his staff and his own tough constitution, he pulled through. Mr Knox sold him as a yearling to Mr William Disney of Lark Lodge, the Curragh, who owned and trained him throughout his racing career.

Described as a graceful light-actioned chestnut, Birdcatcher was slow to mature. He had only one race as a two-year old, the Paget Plate at the Curragh, which he failed to win. His first outing in the next season was in the Madrid Stakes at the Curragh. In this race he demonstrated his great speed, a characteristic he was to pass on to his descendants. He won easily from a filly, Maria, who was claimed to be the best of her sex in Ireland. He followed this with another victory in the Milltown Stakes and with a head defeat by Maria, who, with an advantage in the weights, just turned the tables on him.

So far, though he had shown speed and promise, he had not accomplished anything outstanding. His next race was the Peel Challenge Cup, which was run over 1¾ miles of 'the severest course at the Curragh'. Established in 1819 and named in honour of Sir Robert Peel, the Cup was then one of the principal events in the Irish racing calendar. In it he was opposed by the best that Ireland could produce, the field including Freney, winner of twenty-seven races and described as 'a superlative performer who has swept all before him at the Curragh'. Freney was owned by a Mr R. H. Copperthwaite, 'a rascally Dublin solicitor', of whom we shall hear again. Both Freney and another crack, Normandy, were well fancied to beat Birdcatcher.

Setting off in front from the moment the flag fell, not only was Birdcatcher never headed, he was never seriously challenged, the winning verdict being given as 'over five hundred yards'. After passing the post he was still so full of running that his jockey could not pull him up. He bolted and did not stop until he reached the cavalry barracks at Newbridge — nearly two miles, most of it on the hard high road.

This was his greatest performance, and Mr Disney would have been well advised to rest him then, especially after the hammering he had received on the road. Instead he pulled him out again the following day and then ran him once more at the next Curragh meeting. Not surprisingly he was beaten each time. That race for the Peel Cup, coupled with what occurred after it and his owner's insistence on running him so soon, unquestionably affected his great speed. In addition, in the opinion of Joseph Osborne, one of the leading authorities of the day, who witnessed the race, it also affected his staying power. In the next season he won three races and was placed in three others, one of these defeats being in the Northumberland Plate, when he went down to the year younger Harkaway, to whom he was attempting to concede no less than 20lb. He lost nothing in this defeat save the race, and had he been the horse he was before the Peel Cup, he might well have succeeded in beating his great rival despite the weight concession.

Whether Birdcatcher is entitled to enter the ranks of truly great racehorses is, on his performances, open to question, yet he did undeniably touch true greatness once in that race for the Peel Cup. It brooks no argument, however, that he can claim immortality in his achievements as a sire of winners and dams of winners. Before dealing with these it is necessary to trace the career of his mighty successor on the Turf, the colt who had defeated him in the Northumberland Plate — Harkaway.

4

Harkaway was bred and owned by one of the most extraordinary characters ever to enter the pages of Irish racing history. Tom Ferguson commenced his career in a linen factory in the north of Ireland. A natural horseman imbued with a love or racing and a desire to excel, he also had an instinctive flair for appraising quality in horseflesh and handling it when he got it. Very soon, therefore, he left the factory to devote his life to horses and racing, 'exchanging calico for silk' as one wag put it. Much of his early race-riding was done in the west, and at that stage of his career he was a genial outgoing man who possessed all the qualities of a boon companion. In no time at all his abilities as a race-rider and his charm of manner had won for him a place in the hearts — and houses — of the hardy sportsmen of Galway and Mayo. He was taken up by the Lords Cremorne and Clanmorris, for both of whom he rode; they introduced him to others with whom he was equally successful, and when he said 'I know all the lords, ye see,' it was not an idle boast.

An immensely strong rider who rode very short by the standards of the time, he was the equal of any of the cracks of the day across a country, and it was said that not even the McDonough brothers, then ranked as the best among gentlemen riders, could afford to give him a yard of distance or a pound of weight in a race. Ferguson unashamedly rode for the plunder and was not too scrupulous about how he obtained it. In 1839, Lottery's year, he ran three horses in the Grand National: Rust, an entire horse, the mount on which he gave to Willie McDonough; Daxon, whom he rode himself; and Barkston, ridden by a professional, Larry Byrne. Rust, described as 'the best-looking horse in the field', appears to have been the fancied runner of the three.

At the brook the second time round Ferguson was upsides with the redoubtable Captain Becher on Conrad, who, it seems, was going rather too well for Ferguson's peace of mind. No one knows just what happened, except that the two horses rose at the fence together and when they landed Becher was in the brook while Ferguson was galloping on. Ferguson, therefore, if he had no other claim to fame, will at least go down in history as having an important part in the christening of the famous fence. Becher, incidentally, is said to have shouted from the brook as his rivals jumped over him: 'It's damn cold stuff without brandy in it!'

The incident did Ferguson little good, for he fell himself shortly afterwards. Rust, however, continued full of running and looked all over a winner until, according to a contemporary, 'the other jockeys manoeuvred him down a lane and kept him there until they were well clear'. Ferguson's protests at this treatment were loud, clear and increasingly vehement, but they were of no avail, for Lottery was declared the winner, while Rust appears in the records as 'pulled up'.

None of these escapades and many others like them intefered with Ferguson's popularity amongst the nobility and gentry west of the Shannon, many of whom were just as hard on their horses and their opponents as he was. Harkaway's dam, Fanny Dawson, was in fact given to him as a present by Lord Cremorne and was named by her new owner in honour of one of his lordship's daughters.

5

In view of Harkaway's subsequent pre-eminence as a racehorse and his importance to the Irish Turf in this period, it is necessary to set out the story of his breeding in some detail.

In 1793 Mr Edwards, a Yorkshireman who had settled at Brownstown House, the Curragh, some years before, mated one of his mares with Tom Tug, a stallion he had himself imported, having bought him from the Duke of Grafton. Tom Tug carried the Herod blood and had been a successful racehorse, winning on ten occasions from twenty-five starts. This mating produced a colt subsequently named Commodore, who won no less than six King's Plates in two years. When retired to stud Commodore became a prolific sire of winners, amongst whom was Irish Escape, who has already been mentioned in Birdcatcher's pedigree and who was described by a contemporary as one of the best horses ever to run at the Curragh. Of more immediate importance from the point of view of this story, Commodore also got Rugatino, and in turn when put to stud Rugatino got the oddly named Nabocklish, who, after winning four King's Plates, was bought by Lord Cremorne to stand at his stud in Co. Monaghan.

At about this time Mr Jason Hessard, a landowner and sportsman from Co. Fermanagh, hired a freighter to take a cargo of bullocks to the Liverpool market. Having disposed of these at a satisfactory price, he journeyed to Knowsley, where he purchased from Lord Derby a well-bred filly, Miss Tooley, who was out of a half-sister to an Oaks winner. Returning with her as his sole cargo, he sold the unraced filly at a profit to a Mr Dawson, a relative of Lord Cremorne. She won several good races for Mr Dawson and soon attracted the attention of Lord Cremorne. He purchased her, and after she had won the Mare's Plate at the Curragh for him in the following year he sent her to his stud, where she was put to Nabocklish. The result was the filly Fanny Dawson, whom Lord Cremorne presented to Tom Ferguson.

By the time Fanny Dawson came to be mated Ferguson himself had come south and established himself at Rossmore Lodge on the Curragh. Having received the mare as a present, he returned the compliment by sending her to Lord Cremorne's stallion Economist. The result of this mating was a colt foal born in April 1834 whom he named Harkaway.

At first Ferguson did not think much of the foal, who was leggy and ungainly, and he sent him off to the farm of Mr Thomas McEvoy in Westmeath to run with his cattle. For nearly two years he remained there, out at grass and half-forgotten until Ferguson suddenly remembered his existence. He brought him in, hurriedly broke him and ran him in the Anglesey Stakes at the Curragh in 1836. Quite unready and hardly half-fit, Harkaway was soundly beaten. The rest of his two-year-old career was undistinguished save for a victory in the Constantine Stakes at the Curragh, where he showed blinding speed and served some notice of what was to come.

It was as a three-year-old that Harkaway began to come into his own. In that year, as has already been mentioned, he beat Birdcatcher in the Northumberland Plate, with Freney too, amongst other good horses, well beaten behind him. Thenceforward, knowing what he had to bet on, Ferguson made full use of him. He ran at every Curragh meeting during the following year, suffering only one defeat. Altogether between September 1836 and June 1838 he contested twenty-three races at the Curragh and won eighteen of them. These victories were made even more noteworthy by the substantial weight concessions which he was giving away to the beaten horses.

Ferguson not only rode for the plunder, he trained for it and took no pains to disguise the fact. Indeed he advertised his intentions at the top of a powerful and penetrating voice. His transgressions, which were many, were carried out quite openly. In a race at Blackrock Strand, near Newry, when the townspeople had forestalled him in the market by backing his fancied mount, Barkston, he laid against him and then rode him into the sea, in full view of spectators and stewards, as the best means of stopping him.

At the end of the 1838 season he decided that the Irish betting market was not strong enough to accommodate the weight of his money. 'It's just not worthwhile here to rob,' he announced to anyone who cared to listen. 'There is not a butcher in Liverpool

Harkaway.

who would not make more in one throw over a match for a pony than the greatest robber of all would in Ireland if he began with the Kirwans in June and ended with the Rossmore Handicap in October.'

By this time Ferguson was suffering terribly from gout and his once genial temperament had turned sour. His explosions of temper earned for him the name of 'Choleric Tom'. He became, too, ever more hard on his great horse, eccentric, to say the least, in his methods of obtaining the price he wanted when he ran, and virulently outspoken about those against whom he had conceived the more violent of his many dislikes.

Space does not allow Harkaway's English career to be set down in any detail. Suffice it to say that he started in fifteen races, most of them against top-class opponents, and won eight of them, the majority of his seven defeats being brought about by his owner to suit the state of his betting book. His victories established without question his claim to greatness. He won two Goodwood Cups, the first much as he liked from a high-class field, and this after pulling up lame at Liverpool a fortnight before, Ferguson having run him twice in successive days in an effort to recoup earlier losses. His second Goodwood Cup in the following year was probably the finest performance of his great career. Over a distance of 2¾ miles, carrying 9st 4lb and giving weight all round except to Epirus, who was rated the best of his age in England, he came home an easy winner in a time of under five minutes. The runner-up was receiving no less than 36lb, and the third, Deception, winner of that season's Oaks, 29lb. Epirus was beaten a distance. Harkaway started favourite at even money, much of which, needless to say, was Ferguson's. To increase the day's takings he sold the Gold Cup back to the executive, who had it run for again on the following day under the name of the Harkaway Cup!

Not surprisingly Ferguson's tirades against those who crossed him, coupled with the unconcealed in-and-out running of his horses, did not endear him to the racing authorities on either side of the Irish Sea. His most hated enemy was Lord George Bentinck, the self-styled dictator of the English Turf, who, in his own patrician way, was every bit as dishonest in his betting as was Ferguson. In 1838, when Harkaway won the Chesterfield Cup, Bentinck somehow succeeded in obtaining the best price and clamping the odds before Ferguson could get his own money on. Furiously Ferguson announced at the top of his voice as Harkaway passed the post: 'I've got the Chesterfield Stakes and I'll get more, but, by God, the public must understand that Harkaway is my horse, to win money for me, and not for any damned fellow, either a lord or a lord by courtesy and a thief by the curse of God!'

Bentinck several times tried to buy Harkaway, offering large sums which were refused in terms which contemporary chroniclers dared not commit to print. The victory of Harkaway's which gave Ferguson the greatest satisfaction of all was at Cheltenham when his great horse slammed Bentinck's Grey Momus, winner of the Two Thousand Guineas, the St Leger, the Ascot Gold Cup and other good races. 'That fellow with the buttons [which was one of the milder epithets he employed in referring to his lordship] knows me now,' he declared in stentorian tones, looking up at his enemy from the foot of the Jockey Club stand. 'And he won't like spancelling the kicking Irishman, I think.'

Lord George Bentinck was not the only person wishing to buy Harkaway. Enquiries flowed in from all over the world. To one from America Ferguson replied: 'The price is six thousand guineas, and I hunt him twice a week!'

What feats Harkaway might have achieved under more sympathetic handling can only be conjectured. His owner's undisguised cheating led to his horse being allotted far greater weights in handicaps than would have normally been the case, yet in many instances he triumphed over them. The pundits of the English sporting press were, not without justification, uniformly hostile to both the horse and his owner, yet the *Sporting Magazine*, the most critical of them all, could not refrain from commenting after Harkaway's second Gold Cup: 'When the time in which the race was run is considered it proves, not only that Harkaway is the best racer in the world, but it is a long time since we had such a combination of speed and stoutness in one animal.' And the great authority Joseph Osborne described him as 'the grandest and best horse I have ever seen in my long career on and off the Turf'.

In appearance Harkaway, who stood about 16 hands, exhibited more power than quality; in fact he has been variously described as being 'ungainly' and 'on the leg', but he had impressive shoulders and his quarters were immensely strong, so much so that when galloping his thighs came up with such force that they would frequently brush the legs of his jockey.

Harkaway was not an outstanding success at stud, but he did get King Tom, who sired St Angela, the dam of St Simon. The initial fee for his services demanded by Ferguson was 100 guineas, a huge sum for a stallion in those days, and he failed to fill. After standing at Rossmore Lodge for a season he was sent by Ferguson to Newmarket, where the fee was reduced to 30 guineas. Then Ferguson brought him back to Rossmore Lodge, where he stood him at a fee of 31 guineas. He remained at the Curragh until his owner's death, when he was sold to Mr David Robinson of Ladykirk, Berwickshire. He died in Februrary 1859.

It has to be said in Ferguson's defence that in the manner of his cheating he was in many respects no worse than his social superiors. In 1842, the year Harkaway was retired to stud, Lord Howth, charitably described by one Turf historian as 'having a weakness for pulling off a coup', entered his Morpath for the Queen's Plate at Bellewstown, which was then run in two heats. There were four runners in the first heat, and at the last bend the second horse, Pickpocket, carried the other two runners out of the course, letting Morpath through on the rails to win. Exactly the same thing happened in the next heat, and Morpath was declared the winner of the Plate. However, the article of the race stated that no entry would be accepted from the owner of more than one horse 'either in his own name or in trust'. Since the owners of the other runners had reason to believe that Lord Howth owned Pickpocket as well as the winner, an objection followed.

On being called upon to answer the charge, Lord Howth swore an oath administered by Mr James Matthews of Hanover that he had no interest whatever in Pickpocket. Confronted with this sworn evidence, the stewards had no alternative but to allow him to keep the race.

Ten days later Lord Howth ran Pickpocket in his own name at his own meeting, the Howth Park Races. Enquiries were promptly set afoot by those responsible for organising the Bellewstown meeting, and it was then revealed that the name given as the owner of Pickpocket in the entry for the Queen's Plate at Bellewstown was that of Lord Howth's training-groom. A pillar of the Turf Club, Lord Howth was in no way abashed by this disclosure, and at the next Bellewstown meeting was observed quaffing champagne with 'a most useful member of your bench of magistrates'. In the following year, having changed Pickpocket's name to Old Ireland, he ran him as his own in the Chester Cup.

Mr Copperthwaite, the 'rascally solicitor' who has been mentioned in connection with his good horse Freney, was not far behind either of these two gentlemen. One of the favoured methods of cheating in those days concerned the whip with which jockeys weighed out and in. It became the practice amongst the unscrupulous to use a whip of a substantial size, whose centre could be hollowed out and a tube of mercury inserted to give extra weight. On leaving the scales the jockey changed this weighted whip for a normal one handed to him by an accomplice and, on return, reversed the process, thus being enabled to ride with several pounds less than the declared weight and at the same time deceive the clerk of the scales. Mr Copperthwaite, if he was not the originator of this stratagem, was certainly believed to employ it extensively. His nemesis came after an even more ingenious piece of cheating. In 1852 in a race at the Curragh the horse he had entered was opposed by a good three-year-old with a bad action. His intelligence service was always efficient, and he found out that this colt had been tried a certainty. Because of his doubtful forelegs he was to run in ankle boots. Somehow he persuaded the horse's attendant to put on underneath the ankle boots bandages so tight that they completely impeded his action. In the race the horse could barely hobble and was, of course, well beaten. The fraud was only discovered some time after unsaddling. It was never quite brought home to Copperthwaite, but it was so universally accepted that he was the culprit that shortly afterwards he took himself, his string and his stud — which was an extensive one — to England, where he later died poor and friendless.

7

To return, however, from owners to horses, Birdcatcher's career at stud must be briefly dealt with. Although he could not match Harkaway's successes on the racecourse, his achievements as a sire far exceeded those of the greater racehorse, for he became one of the most prepotent and successful stallions of all time. It would require far more space than is here available to enumerate the names and feats of his progeny. If his first few years at stud are alone taken into account, his record is singularly impressive. Almost at the outset of his career he got a Derby winner in Daniel O'Rourke, and two winners of the St Leger, Knight of St George and The Baron, the latter being bred almost by chance. Mr Watts of Jockey Hall offered his dam, Echidna, who never ran, to a priest for £20 to get rid of her. When this was refused he put her to Birdcatcher. She threw The Baron, who won the St Leger so easily that the owner of the second objected, unsuccessfully, on the grounds that such an easy winner must surely be a four-year-old. Others of Birdcatcher's early crops were two winners of the Oaks, Songstress and Imperieuse.

These were only the beginning, for Birdcatcher's descendants were prepotent too. The Baron got Stockwell, 'emperor of stallions'; Stockwell got Doncaster and Bend Or, both Derby winners; and Bend Or sired Ormonde, one of the greatest racehorses of all time. These names only touch on the strengths of the great line he founded. In 1860 he fell when covering a mare called Queen Bee — originally owned by Mr Copperthwaite, who had parted with her for 30 guineas to the Dunne family — and sustained such severe injuries that he had to be put down.

The careers of these two great horses, Birdcatcher and Harkaway, demonstrated to the world that Irish breeding and Irish racehorses could hold their own anywhere. They also in themselves illustrate the evolution of the Irish thoroughbred and take the story of Irish flat racing up to the second half of the nineteenth century.

4

Early Grand Nationals and Lord Waterford

1

During the first half of the nineteenth century considerable progress was being made in developing the steeplechasing branch of the sport. Its home at this time lay chiefly in the west. There was racing at Kiltulla in Galway in 1821, and meetings at this venue continued at intervals until 1867, a steeplechase being invariably included in the programme. In the 1830s a Mayo Spring Meeting took place, extending over three days. Here the steeplechase course covered a distance of four miles. Its articles laid down that three-year-olds carried 9st, and the remainder catchweights. The obstacles were graded, showing that already some thought was being given to the limits of endurance of both men and horses. On the first day there were to be six five-foot walls; on the second the height would be reduced to four feet six inches, and on the third to four feet. There appear to have been intermediate natural obstacles, but no details are given of these.

In 1834 there were meetings at both Ballinrobe and Tuam, and steeplechases were included in their programmes. A year earlier the New Melton Stakes at Cahir was organised by the gentlemen of the district. The course, which was laid out under their super-vision, was described as 'all grass, three miles, thirty-two fences'. At the conclusion of the meeting no fewer than 120 persons sat down to dinner, the company including Lords Waterford, Clanricarde and Clonmel, Mr John Preston, owner of the famous mare Brunette, and Mr Augustus Moore.

The courses at these meetings were all 'out and back', i.e. the riders went away as best they could, rounded a flag at a designated point, and made the best of their way home. The finish was a loosely roped-off passage through the crowd; mounted stewards and hunt servants armed with whips stationed themselves along this route and tried, often vainly, to keep it clear for the horses. Harry S.

Sargent, who had unrivalled knowledge of the developing sport and who has left one of the best descriptions of it, wrote:

> As soon as the leading horse passed everyone closed in, unmindful of those behind, which had either to charge the crowd or be pulled up. I saw many a man ridden over, nearly all were hurt, while some were killed outright. Collisions between the racing horses and those ridden by the stewards or servants, causing terrible disasters, were also of frequent occurrence.

This lack of control inevitably led to malpractices: friends of fancied horses would knock holes in fences, or they would deliberately interfere with their rivals out in the country far from the view of such stewards as there were; mounted 'helpers' would be installed at the various obstacles, ready to catch loose horses or give a lead to recalcitrant jumpers.

The sport was nevertheless attracting large crowds, drawn mostly from the rural population. Sargent says:

> Every fence and vantage-point was thronged with frieze-coated farmers, their sons and labourers. Within a ten-mile radius of the course not one of them could be found at home, except those too ill or too old. Wherever was a fence more formidable than the others there would congregate the crowd in greatest numbers. Every man evinced the keenest interest in the sport, which was intensified when a neighbour's horse ran, and if he won the excitement amounted to a frenzy.

Much the same could be said of what was happening in England, but the more orderly English crowds soon began to demand the suppression of at least the worst of the evils prevalent in races run over ill-defined courses, and they also insisted on a better opportunity for viewing the racing. The result was the first steeplechase run over an enclosed course; this significant event took place at Liverpool in 1836. No such innovation was to be introduced in Ireland for many years to come, and Sargent further records that

> The courses were laid out over a perfectly natural country; not a single sod or stone would be removed nor a fence trimmed, and there was no levelling of places where the going was bad. . . . The course would be laid out a few days beforehand, and nothing further done but put up the flags on the morning of the races.

He goes on to say that there were no stands, or 'stand-houses' as they were called, save at a few meetings, and these, such as they were, were primitive in the extreme and reserved for the gentry who paid an entrance fee 'not exceeding five shillings'. Dressing-rooms and weighing-rooms did not exist. Occasionally a sympathetic executive provided a dressing-tent, but more often the riders changed in the open, and Sargent could recall changing beneath a fence in a rain-storm while a friend held an umbrella over his head. Weighing in and out took place in the open, with all its attendant difficulties and opportunities for unintentional mistakes or deliberate cheating. The betting that took place at these meetings consisted almost entirely of private wagers amongst the gentry. There was only one bookmaker who attended southern meetings. His name was Mullins; his wife acted as his assistant, and his takings were so small that he had to operate a roulette wheel in order to make ends meet.

Lively and informal as these meetings were, the Irish did not overlook the attractions offered by English steeplechasing over the more definitely laid out or, as they deemed them, 'artificial' courses, of which the chief was Liverpool.

2

There is some controversy as to the date on which the first Grand National was run. Some place it in 1837, others in 1839. It does seem established, however, that the Liverpool steeplechases of 1837 and 1838 were not run at Aintree but at Maghull, and therefore do not rank as true 'Grand Nationals'. Be that as it may, the 1838 race was won by Sir William, owned and ridden by Allen McDonough and trained by him in Ireland.

As we have seen, it was in the first Grand Liverpool Steeplechase run at Aintree that Tom Ferguson put Captain Becher into the brook that bears his name. Of the three horses which Ferguson ran in this race, one was ridden off the course and the others fell. Ferguson, in his uninhibited way, blamed these falls on the fact that the fences were not the natural ones the horses had known in Ireland.

Others too took the same view, but this did not deter the Irish from returning again and again to the Aintree meeting. Added attractions were the easy access to Liverpool from Irish ports and a stake which by the standards of the times was very substantial — the 1847 race, for instance, was worth £990 to the winner. The next few years saw entries by Ferguson himself, the Marquis of Waterford, Mr John Power and Lord Howth amongst others, and it was to Mr Power that the honour fell of having Valentine's Brook named after his horse Valentine, which he rode into third place in 1840. He had backed himself for a substantial sum to be first over the wall which then stood in front of the stands in the place where the water-jump is now. To achieve this he set such a cracking pace that he won his bet, but, unable to check his headlong gallop, he only survived the second brook by a miracle, his horse trying to refuse, all but running out, and finally bucking over it in what was described as a 'corkscrew' motion. Thereafter it became known as Valentine's Brook.

The year 1847, when the name of the race was changed from the Grand National Steeplechase to the Grand National Handicap Steeplechase, saw a second Irish victory when Mathew, ridden by Denny Wynne, came home in front of another Irish horse, St Leger. Mathew was bred in Ireland by Mr John Westropp and was owned and trained in Ireland by Mr John Courtenay of Ballyedmond, Co. Cork. Although some records spell his name 'Matthew', the horse had in fact originally been named Father Mathew after the priest who became famous throughout Ireland as a tireless and trenchant campaigner for total abstinence. In addition to Mathew and St Leger, there were two other Irish runners, Saucepan and Brunette.

Brunette was then the star of the Irish steeplechasing world. She was thirteen years of age and on the day of the race was suffering from an infection of the throat; in fact she was only started because of a huge wager on her by her rider, Allen McDonough. After being scarcely able to jump the small preliminary hurdle and being tailed

Brunette.

off passing the stand, she ran on gamely to finish sixth. Bred in Co. Meath by the stallion Sir Hercules, the sire of Birdcatcher, she was the winner of countless races, including the Kilrue Cup, then one of the most important of Irish steeplechases, which she won no less than four times in succession. In winning it in 1846 she had soundly beaten both Mathew and St Leger. Her most notable achievement in this race, however, was in 1843, when she slammed Peter Simple, an English crack from the Midlands who had been brought over specially for the occasion. (He should not be confused with the Peter Simple who won the Grand Nationals of 1849 and 1853.) Allen McDonough had the mount on Peter Simple, and he had struck a series of bets on his chances — an even £50 that he would not refuse, another even £50 that he would not fall, and an even £100 that he would win. Ridden by her owner, Mr Preston, Brunette was headed ten lengths at the last fence. Such was her finishing speed that she got up to beat the leading horse, Milo, by a length, Peter Simple running into third place another length behind. Mr Preston thought so much of her and ran her so often that he had a special horse-drawn van built to convey her from meeting to meeting all over Ireland. Railways being then in their infancy, the usual method of travelling horses was to walk them from their quarters to the course, a process which often took days and was, according to one writer of the time, 'attended by various perils'.

St Leger confirmed the value of Mathew's 1847 victory by going to France and becoming the first Irish horse to win the Grand Steeplechase de Paris. In the Aintree race Mathew had been heavily backed by the huge Irish contingent which had come over to support him. Their bacchanalian celebrations on the packets returning home did little to further the cause of the man after whom he had been originally named, and the current smart saying in racing circles was that if he had not won, half Ireland would have had to emigrate.

In fact half Ireland — or very near it — *had* emigrated, for these were the terrible famine years. The famine, however, scarcely touched upon the rich and the landed, save in some cases to make their rents less secure. They were therefore able to continue their sporting pursuits undisturbed by the ghastly scenes about them, and, so far as racing was concerned, its progress was impeded only in the west and the poorer parts of the country.

3

Not all the great landlords were unmindful of their duties towards the poor and the afflicted. Amongst the most prominent of those who showed some concern for the welfare of their tenants was

Painting the town red.

Sporting Exploits of a Noble Marquis.

The Noble Marquis on his Celebrated Hunter Don Juan, jumping a five barred Gate in a Drawing Room at Melton for a bet of 100 Guineas at half past Woclock at Night in December with a Blazing Fire staring him in the Face.

Henry, third Marquis of Waterford. His youth had been a wild one, commencing with the successful spiriting away from Eton of Keate's notorious 'flogging block' and its removal to the family seat at Curraghmore, where it is still preserved. At Melton, where he rode as hard and as straight as anyone and harder and straighter than most, he earned for himself the nickname of the 'Wild Marquis'. Along with some of his swell friends he originated the term 'painting the town red' from an exploit depicted by Henry Alken, the sporting artist, and entitled by him 'Spree at Melton Mowbray, or Doing the Thing in a Sporting-like Manner'. When aged nineteen he matched his horse Cock Robin against Captain Lambe's Vivian for £2,000. Bred in Ireland, Vivian was then held to be one of the best steeplechasers in England, and Lambe secured the services of Captain Becher to ride him. The match was run over four miles of natural country near Melton Mowbray. Unlucky in the running and in the line he took, Waterford was beaten two lengths. 'Where is the man', an enthusiastic chronicler of the time recorded, 'that ever was, or ever will be, to ride as the loser of that race did, *with a Marquisate and £50,000 a year to cool his courage*? What splendid promise of future excellence does this achievement in a 19th year afford?'

Henry, third Marquis of Waterford, in his 'Wild Marquis' youth, jumping a five-barred gate in a Melton drawing room for a bet of a hundred guineas with, according to the original caption, 'a blazing fire staring him in the face'.

37

When he returned home to Curraghmore in 1840, the same year that he rode his own horse The Sea in the Grand National and started another runner in it, the Marquis amply fulfilled this prophecy. In 1844 he took over the mastership of the Waterford Foxhounds, which he hunted himself at his own expense and with resounding success for the rest of his life. Soon he was one of the pillars of Irish racing, not only as an owner and rider but also as a administrator, becoming a sort of benevolent dictator of the Turf, using every effort in a quiet and undemonstrative way to exercise control and check excesses. As evidence of the scale on which he supported the sport, it may be noted that when he died he had 152 nominations in Irish races and nine in England. A year seldom passed without his having one or more runners in the Grand National. The nearest he came to winning was when his Sir John, ridden by his stud-groom Johnny Ryan 'the Jock', finished third in the successive years 1850 and 1851.

Johnny Ryan had come to Lord Waterford's service from the Curragh and remained with him for fifty years, a rare tribute to both master and man. As well as turning his horses out in superlative condition, as a rider he won 112 races for his master, amongst them the Autumn Steeplechase at Liverpool on Sir John, the Metropolitan Steeplechase at Epsom, and numerous races both on the flat and over the fences at Cashel, Tipperary, Howth and the Curragh.

There was at this time a private course at Curraghmore for trials and schooling, and for a short time William I'Anson, later to gain fame as the trainer of Blink Bonny and Caller Ou, trained the Waterford horses, assisted by Johnny Ryan. Captain Edward Peel rode the Corinthian races. He too was a brilliant horseman, but no one could ever tell exactly how many races he won, since his services were so much in demand that he had to have frequent recourse to assumed names so as to avoid bringing down the wrath of his military superiors upon him for his absences from duty.

Nor did Lord Waterford, in the midst of all the calls on his time, fail his tenantry as so many of his fellows did. He was a benevolent and improving landlord. During the famine he laid out money lavishly on schemes to provide work and alleviate distress. A memorialist, writing some years after his death from a fall out hunting in 1859, summed him up aptly in the following passage:

Still we read frequent mention of the 'Wild Marquis', of the mad exploits of his youth, when with other kindred spirits he 'heard the chimes at midnight', of his steeplechases and single combats, but never a word is said in print of those seventeen years of exemplary married life when he resided entirely on his estates and among his people, doing good to all, warding off starvation with a generous hand during the famine years, and by his vast employment of labour and his practical encouragement of agriculture and industries nobly fulfilling the duties of a great country gentleman.

Henry, third Marquis of Waterford, at work at his desk at Curraghmore.

5

Enter Lord Drogheda

1

The decade immediately following the famine saw striking developments both on the flat and over the fences. In steeplechasing the Irish horse began to establish the ascendancy he has never lost when Abd-el-Kader won the Grand National in the successive years 1850 and 1851, a feat which was not to be repeated until Reynoldstown, another Irish-bred, won in 1935 and 1936. A small horse standing little over 15 hands, 'Little Ab', as his owner affectionately called him, was a brilliant jumper and had no difficulty with the formidable obstacles. He was bred by Mr Henry Osborne of Davidstown Castle, Drogheda, who bought his dam when travelling from London to Holyhead on the 'Shrewsbury Hirondelle' coach. As he watched the action of the horses drawing the coach the near leader caught his eye as being a good one to breed from. On making enquiries he found who her breeder was and, searching him out, obtained from him an affidavit that she was by Hit or Miss out of a half-bred mare. Armed with this information, he went to her owner and purchased her for 50 guineas. His judgment was not at fault. Named Irish Lass, she won steeplechases for him and, when put to stud, bred a succession of winners. Her ninth foal, a colt by Ishmael, was named by him Abd-el-Kader. The colt displayed such a savage temperament that he was judged useless for flat racing and was gelded, but so severe were the effects of the operation that he almost died. His recovery was slow, and he was put by for two years. Then, taken out hunting preparatory to being put to steeplechasing, he sustained another injury which nearly killed him. Nursed back to health, he won his first steeplechase at Worcester and, despite his size, went on to be one of the best steeplechasers in the United Kingdom.

By the time he scored his successive victories in the Grand National Abd-el-Kader had passed into the ownership of Mr Osborne's

Abd-el-Kader, winner of the Grand National in 1850 and 1851.

son Joseph, who has already been mentioned as a noted authority on breeding and whose monumental *Horse Breeder's Handbook* (1881) became and remained for many years the definitive work on the subject. He was also the owner and compiler of the *Steeple-chase Calendar* and a frequent contributor of articles on racing and breeding subjects to *Bell's Life in London*, a leading sporting magazine.

It is worth noting too that in 1850, the year that saw Abd-el-Kader's first victory, the horses who occupied the first, second and third places in the race were all Irish bred, owned and trained, and indeed, with the exception of Sam Darling's mount, Tipperary Boy, also Irish ridden.

The year 1855 saw another Irish victory. The winner was Wanderer, who earned the distinction of being the first stallion to win the race, though he had little else to commend him. Described as a 'rough, undersized, common-loking hunter', he was only started as a lead horse for his stablemate, Boundaway, who carried all his owner's money; and the race itself was generally accepted as being of the lowest standard for many years.

2

At home the good old days and ways of early steeplechasing were still being perpetuated. A testimony to these is provided by Major

William Trocke, the son of a parson from Ormond, Co. Tipperary, who became one of the leading riders in the country, winning amongst countless other races the Conyngham Cup on Mr Harper's mare Olympia and completing his career by winning the Prince of Wales's Plate at Punchestown in 1904 at the age of sixty-seven. Having learnt the rudiments of steeplechase riding when in his teens from John Hubert Moore, he was able to remember that when he began, in the 1850s, races were run in two-mile heats, and, he says, horses frequently had to cover eight or ten miles before a decision was reached.

> The courses [he continues] were often laid over the stiffest line that could be selected. I have seen a stone and mortar wall in one, and stone-faced banks five or six feet high were considered most suitable fences. I remember, in 1856, seeing John Hubert Moore, riding a match, carrying eighteen stone, over the Knockbarron course in Galway, where all the jumps were four-and-a-half-feet walls; and I have a distinct recollection of what riding at the last of them on a beaten horse was like.

Trocke goes on to say that the riding in those days was of 'the very roughest description'. He tells how a jockey he knew, riding in a race where there were only two runners, caught his opponent by the collar of his jacket at a part of the course entirely hidden from view of spectators or stewards and, pulling him out of the saddle, went on to win as he liked.

> Keeping the course [Trocke observes, echoing Sargent's words] was a duty almost entirely neglected. I remember riding in a military race at Newbridge, where the steeplechase course was inside the flat. The crowd thought there was another round of the steeplechase course to be taken, and stood in a dense mass on the flat course just beyond the judge's box. I was riding a mare belonging to David Palesy, the well-known veterinary of the RA: poor Bay Middleton was on a horse of his own, and Frank Osborne on a very smart mare named Clitonia. It was a very close finish between the three. As soon as we passed the post there was nothing in it but to gallop right into the dense crowd, which we accordingly did, as there was not time to pull up, and I have a vivid recollection of seeing poor Bay and his horse turning about three somersaults among the crowd. We picked ourselves up and weighed in, and, strange to say, no one was killed, nor, so far as I can remember, even seriously injured. They do these things better now.

As it happened, they were even then in the process of doing so, for the sport was beginning to evolve from the haphazard, happy-go-lucky atmosphere of the thirties and forties into the embryo of what we know today.

42

The most important event of the decade, so far as steeplechasing was concerned, was the inaugural meeting at Punchestown. There had been racing of a sort there since the mid-1840s, but it was not until 1854 that the meeting was put on a proper footing and two days allotted to it. The occasion has been preserved for posterity by Michael Angelo Hayes's picture 'The Corinthian Cup', which depicts not only the runners and riders but also many of the leading Irish racing personalities of the day. Although the racing was over a defined circuit, the fences remained natural ones, and the amenities were as primitive as ever, there being only a small wooden 'stand-house' for the accommodation of spectators. Things, however, were about to change.

3

In the year 1860 there came into prominence for the first time in the person of Henry, third Marquis of Drogheda, a successor to Lord Waterford as the benevolent and beloved leader of the Irish Turf. Like his predecessor, he was not an absentee but a resident landlord at his seat, Moore Abbey, where he managed his estate, cared for his tenants and devoted his time, his activities and his purse to the furthering of local interests and institutions. It was at his instigation that in 1861 Punchestown Races were reorganised and reconstituted, becoming known under the title they have borne ever since — 'The Kildare and National Hunt Steeplechases'. Assisted by the advice of Mr Thomas Waters, a professional racing engineer who was also responsible for Tramore and Cork Park, permanent stands were built and enclosures laid out. Nor was the course itself neglected, for Waters was called in to help here too, though to the satisfaction of the diehards the fences were left in their natural condition or very near it, 'a little trimming' being all that was permitted.

The Conyngham Cup course, as it was known then and until very recently, was first opened and used in 1862 when the National Hunt Steeplechase was run over it. The famous 'big double' was included in this first running and has, in one form or another, been jumped at the Punchestown Spring Meeting ever since. In 1863 the Marquis of Downshire presented a silver cup for a welter race, for which a special course was laid out. Known as the Downshire Course, it included as its second fence a formidable four-and-a-half-foot wall which, though considerably modified, also remained as an obstacle until recent years.

Fairyhouse was another racecourse which came into existence at the middle of the century. The year 1851 saw the Ward Union Hunt Races being moved from Ashbourne to their present situation. Once more the country crossed was a natural one, thus preserving the

Henry, third Marquis of Drogheda.

44

tradition of the Kilrue Cup, which was described as being run over 'a well-selected country lying between the Fairy House and the Black Ball about twelve miles from Dublin — a country all grass excepting two ploughed fields, with fourteen fair fences'.

In 1864 the immediate precursor of the Galway Plate was run at Knockbarron, near Loughrea. This was the Western Plate, value £200, the riders to be 'Gentlemen Riders qualified for National Hunt Races at Punchestown or members of the County Galway Hunt'. The Ballybrit course itself was opened five years later on 17 August 1869. It owed its inception to the foresight, drive and organising ability of Lord St Lawrence, MP for Galway, who employed Thomas Waters to lay out the course and design the stands. The chief race, then as now, was 'The Galway Plate of 100 sovs, an open handicap steeplechase. Distance 2½ miles over the steeplechase course. Weights not less than 9st 0lb.' The circuit was a mile and a half 'covered with herbage or moss', and there were eight fences on the circuit, two of which were stone walls. At that first meeting there were thirteen runners, and the race was won by Mr Bell's Absentee, ridden by W. Bell.

Concessions regarding entry money were given to local owners. Lord St Lawrence arranged for special trains to take holiday-makers to the course and also organised a boat service from Cong across Lough Corrib. There was also a proviso that the directors of the Midland and Great Western Railway would convey all horses to and from the racecourse without charge, *provided* they had run in a race.

Everything went off like clockwork; there were huge crowds, and the whole affair was voted a tremendous success. To make certain that control of the racing was vested in those who knew what they were about, Lord St Lawrence had drawn his stewards from experienced racing and hunting men such as Lord Clanricarde, Lord Clanmorris, Henry S. Persse and Valentine Blake. These, before racing, issued a minatory warning to all jockeys that 'If found guilty of sly practices in riding, they will be at once disqualified and warned off the course,' and mounted officials were appointed to watch the running and report upon it.

These precautions were not out of place, for Harry Sargent comments that except in confined events such as Corinthian and military races or the many 'Red Coat' hunt races still contested in the old way over a chosen line of country (he gives a graphic description of one of these in which he rode), there were very few gentlemen jockeys riding in those days. Previous to the 1870s, he says,

> We had only some five or six 'gentlemen jockeys' in Ireland then — I mean those who rode regular races — but it was customary for them to pay a professional for standing down when they got up, and if this was not done habitually things were made very

unpleasant for the amateur during the running. Poor Captain Shaw found this to his cost in many a race, till finally and *fatally* he found it at Youghal. I think it was Captain Tempest who I saw give Dan Meany £10 for the mount on Blind Harper at Cashel.

The whole question of 'gentlemen jockeys' was in fact one of the scandals of steeplechasing at that time, since in England such practised horsemen as Tom Oliver and Captain Becher and in Ireland Tom Ferguson and the McDonough brothers had assumed the title while riding every bit as well and as often as the best professionals. In addition, any claim they might have made never to have taken money for their services would scarcely have stood up to critical examination. In fact when Brunette was declared to run in a handicap steeplechase at Windsor Allen McDonough, her rider, claimed the 5lb allowance granted by its article to a 'gentleman rider' and substantiated the claim by saying that he was a member of the Irish Turf Club. Lord Drumlanrig, a steward, objected, and the claim was refused.

The practice of 'buying a ride', with all the sinister implications referred to by Sargent, was another of the many malpractices which Lord Drogheda was determined to stamp out. In 1866 he drew up a set of rules for the governance of steeplechasing and of all those who took part in it. Since, however, at that time the Turf Club refused to recognise its sister sport, there was then no governing body to enforce these rules, which could thus be effective, if at all, merely as guidelines for local stewards.

A similar situation existed in England, where the condition of steeplechasing was then far worse than in Ireland. Flagrant abuses and malpractices flourished unchecked and had been allowed to proliferate to an extraordinary degree, in spite of vociferous protests not only from such writers as Nimrod and Surtees but also from leaders of the sport itself. For some years prominent members of the Jockey Club had campaigned for the setting up of a governing body to control the sport. Despite opposition from the more hidebound of its members, amongst them Admiral Rous, the then dictator of the English Turf, who would have preferred to see steeplechasing abolished altogether, wiser counsels eventually prevailed. In 1866 the Grand National Hunt Committee was formed, its rules were recognised by the Jockey Club, and its authority to control the sport and inflict penalties, including 'warning off' and other extreme sanctions, was confirmed.

4

By this time Lord Drogheda was occupying in Ireland much the same position as head of the Turf as Admiral Rous did in England, though he used his powers in a far less despotic way. He was thus well situated to insist that Ireland should follow England's example, and in 1869 he met with little opposition when he formulated his proposals for the setting up of the Irish National Hunt Steeplechase Committee. The names of seventeen gentlemen prominent in the sport put forward by him as the first committee members were accepted without question, and the first meeting of the committee took place the following year at the house of Mr R. J. Hunter, the Keeper of the Match Book, who was nominated to be secretary to the new body.

It was Lord Drogheda who introduced number cloths into Irish racing, and it was he who presided at Punchestown when there was an extraordinary objection in the Irish Grand Military Gold Cup in 1873, though it was the 'Military Stewards' who conducted the subsequent enquiry.

Captain Hugh McCalmont, as he then was, rode his brother's horse, Bel Espoir, in the race and was beaten into second place by Waterford, the mount of Captain 'Bay' Middleton, ADC to Earl Spencer, the Lord Lieutenant, and the future pilot in the hunting field of the Empress of Austria. When they had weighed in Captain McCalmont was told by his friends that Waterford had been incorrectly described on the racecard as 'aged', since he was in fact a six-year-old. Thereupon he objected to the winner on the grounds of misdescription. Objections in military races are unusual at the best of times, but this one, made on purely technical grounds, was all the more astounding since the article of the race required both aged horses and six-year-olds to carry 12st 3lb. There was therefore no question of Waterford having carried a lesser weight than he should have done, and he had beaten Bel Espoir by the handsome distance of six lengths at level weights.

The Military Stewards did not take long in informing McCalmont that they considered his objection frivolous. Nevertheless he pressed his case, and either he reminded them, or Lord Drogheda did, or they remembered themselves, that a similar case known as 'the Lad case' had found its way into the law-courts the previous year after a race at Galway. The judge had then decided that when a horse's age was wrongly given disqualification must follow. Accordingly they found that they had no alternative but to disqualify Middleton's mount, which they did, though with apparent reluctance, issuing the following statement:

An objection was lodged by Captain McCalmont against Waterford being entered as aged and running as a five-year-old last year. The Military Stewards disqualified Waterford as being accidentally described as aged — the right age being six years. The stakes were handed over to the owner of the second horse, Bel Espoir, and they considered the question of bets as being out of their jurisdiction.

Punchestown 1868: the Royal Visit.

Since 'Bay' Middleton was probably the best-known and best-liked soldier rider of his day and an objection in a Grand Military, especially on such slender technical grounds, virtually unheard of, it cannot be said that McCalmont's action and its result met with universal acclaim in sporting circles.

But that Punchestown meeting had its full measure of controversy and sensation. Major Dixon complained of the conduct of Thomas Beasley (of whom much more later) during the race, and Beasley was suspended for the rest of the meeting. Then Mr Bull, the owner and rider of Madame Schneider, the second horse home in the Farmers' Challenge Cup, was persuaded, apparently somewhat

48

For key see pp. 50—51.

against his will, to object to the winner, Allspice, as having won £20 on the flat. Mr Bull's reluctance to object was explained when the stewards looked into his own riding, for it seemed that he had not been anxious to get the race at all. Accordingly they referred the matter to the Senior Stewards, who found that Mr Bull had 'deliberately prevented his mare from winning, and suspended him for life and further directed that he should not be permitted to name, enter or run any horse of which he is either wholly or in part owner for any race whatever'.

Lord Drogheda remained a Steward of the INHSC until his death in 1892. He was, in addition, virtually a permanent Steward of the

Painted by Henry Barraud, Esq.

Published by Tho.

1 Captain Davy (Carabiners)	*19 Colonel Kingscote, C.B. & M.P.*	*37 General Sir Hope Grant, G.C.B.*	*55 Burton Persse, Esq.*
2 Viscount Valentia, 10.ʰ Hussars	*20 Lord Crofton*	*38 Late Geo. H⁹ Moore, Esq. M.P.*	*56 Captain Ricardo, 15.ᵗʰ Hussars*
3 Mervyn Tyntz, Esq. 4.ᵗ Dragoon G.ᵗ	*21 Major O.T. Burne A.D.C. 20.ᵗʰ Reg.ᵗ*	*39 Colonel Bowles, 63.ᵈ Reg.ᵗ*	*57 Hon.ᵇᵉ W.ᵐ H. Fitzwilliam, M.P.*
4 R.A. Oswald, Esq.	*22 Captain Gregory, 15.ᵗʰ Hussars*	*40 Captain Bernard*	*58 Thomas Connolly, Esq. M.P.*
5 Hon.ᵇᵉ Thomas Scott Rifle Brigade	*23 Captain M.ᶜ Calmont, 7.ᵗʰ Hussars*	*4. Viscount Combermere*	*59 H.W.ᵐ Briscoe, Esq.*
6 Archibald Peel, Esq.	*24 Gustavus Lambart, Esq.*	*42 The Baron de Robeck*	*60 Earl of Bective, M.P.*
7 Lord Lurgan, K.P.	*25 G. R. Beresford, Esq.*	*43 Viscount Powerscourt*	*61 Captain Hatton, 1.ᵗ Royal Drag*
8 Hon.ᵇᵉ L. Gerald Dillon	*26 Major Gray*	*44 C. Macdonald Morton, Esq.*	*(on Sergeon the Wonet)*
9 Capt.ⁿ The Hon.ᵇᵉ A.W.F. Greville, M.P.	*27 Major General Sir Arthur Cunynghame, K.C.B.*	*45 Viscount Southwell*	*62 George Bryan, Esq. M.P.*
10 H.W.ᵐ Meredyth, Esq.	*28 Marquis of Hamilton, M.P.*	*46 W.ᵐ De Salis Filgate, Esq.*	*63 Viscount Massareene*
11 Marquis of Clanricarde, K.P.	*29 Lord Henry Lennox, M.P.*	*47 Charles P. Hoffman, Esq.*	*64 Major Wilkin*
12 Late Lord Crofton	*30 Colonel Forster. (Master of the Horse)*	*48 The Earl of Wicklow*	*65 William Jameson, Esq.*
13 Marquis of Conyngham, K.P.	*31 Viscount St. Laurence, M.P.*	*49 Colonel Lake, C.B.*	*66 Sir N.W.ᵐ Throckmorton, Bart*
14 Mich.ᵉˡ Martin & C.K. Doyle.	*32 Marquis of Drogheda, K.P.*	*50 Charles Warburton, Esq.*	*67 A.T. Wodehouse, Esq. R.A.*
15 The late Marquis of Downshire	*33 His Royal Highness The Prince of Wales*	*51 Captain C. Roberts*	*68 Lord Clanmorris*
16 Lord Claud John Hamilton, M.P.	*34 Prince Teck*	*52 Richard Moore, Esq.*	*69 Sir Edward Kennedy, Bart.*
17 Earl of Howth, K.P.	*35 Duke of Manchester*	*53 G. R. Dease, Esq.*	*70 Captain Pigott, Scots Greys*
18 Earl of Clonmell	*36 Duke of Cambridge.*	*54 Sir David Roche, Bart.*	*71 Charles Steel, Esq. 12.ᵗʰ Lancer*
			(on Blarkennans).

50

Engraved by T.S. Sanger. Esq.

Turf Club and was nominated Ranger of the Curragh in 1861, in which position he was instrumental in improving both the course and its amenities. In the actual conduct of racing too he was a reformer and always had an eye towards strengthening the rules. The advertisement for the 1876 Irish Derby carried the following warning:

> It will be necessary for those persons who have registered in assumed names to re-register them; this rule applies NOW equally to steeplechasing as well as flat racing. The fee of 1 sov is to be paid either on registration or re-registration.

And as to gentlemen riders wishing to ride in Corinthian races, the following appeared in the same year:

> The National Hunt Club of 1875 is dissolved. A candidate must receive the vote (sanctioning his admission) of four members of the Irish National Hunt Steeplechase Committee, nor can any gentleman ride for these races until he receives this qualification.

To aid aspiring riders who were not so fortunate as to be acquainted with members of the committee, a note was added that the Keeper of the Match Book had been instructed to endeavour to effect introductions to members, who might vouch for the applicant if satisfied with his qualifications.

In his position as head of the Turf it was Lord Drogheda who in April 1868 welcomed the Prince of Wales to Punchestown during the Prince's state visit to Ireland. On the first day he stayed for four races, including the Prince of Wales's Plate for half-bred horses, and on the second, when the Princess accompanied him, he saw all the races and rode round the course inspecting the fences. He displayed particular interest in the formidable 'big double', which was then attaining much the same renown in Irish steeplechasing as Becher's Brook did in its English counterpart. The visit of the Prince was a tremendous success and conferred such a social cachet on the meeting that it became an essential date in the Irish social calendar, Sargent remarking that ever afterwards Punchestown should be known as 'Princely' Punchestown, thus rivalling 'Royal' Ascot and 'Glorious' Goodwood.

Although he owned many good horses, Lord Drogheda never won a classic race, nor, for that matter, any of the top steeplechases, though his home-bred Philammon was second in the Irish Derby and, kept in training until he was seven, that year won the Liverpool Spring Cup and the Esher Cup at Sandown, while his Westmeath won the Kildare Hunt Cup at Punchestown four times in five years. Sargent, who knew him well, describes him as follows:

> Every man in Ireland who knew even the first rudiments of our sport, has for many years looked upon Lord Drogheda as the

Lycurgus of Irish racing, whether across country or on the flat. He was pre-eminently fitted by nature to govern — no man could have five minutes' conversation with him without being impressed by that fact, while his eye, peculiarly penetrating as it was, evinced the determination that lay within. . . . In addition to assuming the leading part in the legislation of the Irish Turf, he took a front place in watching over some of those for whom that legislation was framed. Malpractice could seldom be carried out at any race meeting which he attended without his detecting it. His eagle sight, assisted by the powerfully strong race-glasses he was wont to carry, readily discerned untrue running, and whenever a delinquency was proved against a man, be he owner, trainer or rider, Lord Drogheda visited him with a punishment fully commensurate with the offence.

No wonder it became common practice to enquire of a meeting where anything untoward took place: 'Was the Marquis there?'

6

Jockeys and Gentlemen

1

Lord Drogheda's reign saw the initial running of the Irish Derby at the Curragh in 1866, the inauguration of which owed much to his encouragement and advice, though he cannot have cared much for the first winner of the event. This was Mr James Cockin, an Englishman, and the leader of a band of raiders who had begun to take advantage of the temporary drop in class amongst runners in Irish races and to 'farm' events at the Curragh and elsewhere.

In 1865 Cockin brought over a colt, Lord Conyngham, and with him won seven Queen's Plates at the Curragh. Encouraged by this he continued his raiding career, returning for the October meeting of the same year: on its first day he won the Queen's Plate over three miles, on the second the Lord Lieutenant's Plate over 1½ miles, and on the third the four-mile Royal Whip. Then in the following year he crowned these successes by winning the first Irish Derby with his colt Selim from a disappointing field of three.

Incensed by these successes, the Stewards of the Turf Club passed a ruling that a horse winning £500 in any one year was barred from competing again that year. This in no way deterred Mr Cockin, who maintained at Hednesford in Staffordshire one of the largest strings in England: he simply brought over other horses. The Stewards then had recourse to making a further ruling, issued in 1868, that in future no horse could compete in Royal Plates, Lord Lieutenant's Plates or the Royal Whip unless it had been trained for the previous six months in Ireland. This move was countered by Mr Cockin purchasing a good filly, Aneroid, who was and had been trained at the Curragh by Pat Doucie and was thus qualified. With her he proceeded to win the Queen's Plate, the Royal Whip and three Royal Plates at the Curragh.

Mr Cockin won the Irish Derby again in 1867 with Golden

Plover; two years later his entry, Melody, started favourite and only went down by a short head to The Scout; finally in 1875, the year before his death, he won the race once more, with Innishowen. In all, despite everything the authorities could do to stop him, he was the leading owner in Ireland seven times during the 1860s. Although he won the Irish Derby three times, probably the best horse he ever owned was Uncas, who never ran in it. By Stockwell out of Mr Cockin's own mare Mountain Deer, Uncas won eleven races in Ireland and England as a two-year-old. Like many other owners of that era, Mr Cockin required his horses to work for his money and their keep. There is little doubt that he ruined Uncas's racing career by running him too often and too far as a two-year-old, for in the following season he was not of much account, winning only two races, and those not very convincingly. But, retired immediately to stud, he soon proved his worth as a sire, getting, amongst others in his first crop, Innishowen, Mr Cockin's third and last Irish Derby winner. Innishowen, it is interesting to note, was out of Aneroid, the filly he had bought to circumvent the Stewards' ruling. Uncas, of whom we shall hear again, sired during his career four winners of the Irish Derby.

For the first six years of its existence the distance of the Irish Derby was an extended mile and six furlongs. The early starts were at the red post, and subsequently the race was run over the Peel Course. In 1872 the distance was reduced to 1½ miles to bring it into line with its Epsom counterpart, the Peel Course being retained. It did not, however, in those early days attract any great degree of support from owners and trainers, and runners were few. In an effort to broaden its appeal its articles were altered in 1874 to give a greater range of weights. The public, aided by improved road and rail communication, gave it their support, and this, taken together with the fact that it was run in the summer when the weather was likely to be more propitious, made it rank as a rival to Punchestown as a social occasion.

Although the Curragh continued to be the main centre and focus of Irish racing, other 'enclosed' meetings were, much to the disapproval of the old guard of steeplechasing enthusiasts, beginning to spring up and, in some cases, to prosper. Baldoyle became the first truly 'enclosed' park course in Ireland, holding its inaugural meeting on 19 and 20 March 1860 under the name of the Howth and Baldoyle Race Meeting. It prospered and was to become an object of envy by other executives in that by being first in the field it had received and kept all the best dates. In 1868 its name was changed to Baldoyle Race Meeting, and in 1874 to Dublin Metropolitan Races. The latter year saw the initial running of the Baldoyle Derby at its May Meeting. Established to rival the Irish Derby at the Curragh, the race was run over 1½ miles, and this, together with the fact that its conditions adhered to the classic formula of fixed ages and weights — three years old, colts 8st 10lb, fillies 8st 7lb, no geldings to enter, no allowances and no penalties — made it a truer test than that at the Curragh, which for some years it eclipsed in importance and popularity amongst owners and trainers. Its first running was won by Mr T. Stephens's Bloomfield, with Mr J. S. Denison's Ben Battle second and Mrs J. A. Cassidy's Pride of Kildare third. Such was the success of Baldoyle that in 1891 it was incorporated under the name of the Metropolitan (Baldoyle) Race Company Ltd, with a capital of £10,000.

As the years went by some of the older meetings, such as Cashel and Newcastle, dropped out, but as they did so others took their place. Tramore, on the old course by the sea ('the rabbit burrow afforded an excellent stand'), Cork Park and Galway were all in existence by the 1870s. There was too a course at Wexford on the recently reclaimed sloblands. Mention should also be made of the Curraghmore Hunt Steeplechases, instituted by Lord Waterford in 1870 at Williamstown, near Waterford, and maintained by his family until the last meeting was held in May 1881. The most famous event to take place at Williamstown was the 'Brothers' Race', run on 30 April 1874. This was a sweepstakes of 100 sovs each, distance three miles, owners up, weights 12st, contested by the three brothers Lords Charles, William and Marcus Beresford. It attracted tremendous interest, and the entire countryside flocked to see it. Lord William was up on Woodlark, Lord Marcus on The Weasel and Lord Charles on Nightwalker. They were started by Tom Waters, who combined his work as racecourse designer with all sorts of official and semi-official racing appointments up and down the country. It was neck-and-neck most of the way until Nightwalker weakened. In the race to the post Lord William and Woodlark just got the verdict by a short head. Sargent, who was there, reports that 'The scene of excitement on Williamstown Course during and after it beggars description. Not a mouth was shut nor a voice lower than its highest pitch.'

2

Just as the courses were changing, new names and faces were becoming prominent in both branches of the sport. The most notable of these as an owner and Turf administrator was Mr C. J. Blake. A member of a distinguished Galway sporting family, Mr Blake was elected to the Turf Club in 1866, becoming a Steward for the first time in 1876. It was under his jurisdiction that the office of Clerk of the Course was instituted and his duties laid down in 1877. Mr Blake's home and training stables were at Heath House, Maryborough, and from there his training-groom Jeffrey, under his supervision, sent out a constant stream of winners both in Ireland and England.

Captain Stamer Gubbins, a veteran of the Crimean War and the elder brother of John Gubbins who was later to become renowned as the owner of Ard Patrick and other great horses, was another to come into prominence both as an owner and breeder. His training establishment was at Mountjoy Lodge, the Curragh, where he had set up Dan Broderick, a former jockey, as his private trainer. It was from Mountjoy Lodge that he sent out Redskin to win the Irish Derby in 1877, the only gelding ever to win the race. Redskin was by Uncas, to whom Captain Gubbins had sent his own mare, Wild Daisy. At the disposal sale of Mr Cockin's horses after his death in 1876 Captain Gubbins had bought Uncas and brought him to the stud which he had founded ten years before at Knockany in Co. Limerick. Here he also stood, amongst other good horses, Xenophon, who got Seaman, winner of the Grand National in 1882.

Captain Gubbins advertised Uncas as follows:

AT THE STUD FARM, KNOCANY, BRUFF
UNCAS — a dark brown horse, 15.3

Combining the most fashionable and at the same time the stoutest blood in the stud-book. Calculated to get horses suitable for either the Turf or the market.

Thoroughbred — £5. Half-bred — £3. Groom's fee — 5s.

It was to Uncas that Henry Linde of Eyrefield Lodge, the Curragh, sent his good mare Highland Mary when he retired her from racing. Linde had good reason to look upon Highland Mary with affection and to put her to the best he could get, for it was she who had set him on the high road to astounding success. Buying her for £25 when he had little enough money to spare, he sent her to Fairyhouse and Punchestown, where, well-backed and ridden by Tommy Beasley, then in his teens, she won for him and gave him his start.

3

Henry Eyre Linde was to blaze his name across the racecourses of Ireland, Great Britain and France, yet his great career as a trainer did not start until he was fairly well into his forties. His connection with the Turf resulted from an unusual set of circumstances. Either because his family had fallen upon evil days or as a result of a disagreement with his father (no one now knows which, though the former is the more likely), he 'went for a soldier' and enlisted in the ranks of a marching regiment. When his time expired he joined the Royal Irish Constabulary, rising to the rank of sergeant. Always fascinated by horse-management, he was soon put in charge of the transport horses of his area. From that he branched out into running a hunting stable. Having acquired some capital from this enterprise which was materially increased by his marriage to a Miss Yelverton, who brought with her a handsome dowry, he left the police and was able to buy back the family home at Eyrefield Lodge, where he set himself up as a trainer of racehorses. Winners both on the flat and over the fences were not long in coming, many of them being ridden by himself, for until increasing weight caused his retirement he was a bold and fearless rider across Fairyhouse and Punchestown. He was a shrewd gambler and dealer too, so that his fortunes rapidly multiplied. When he retired Highland Mary to stud he named her first foal Eyrefield. Immediately after Eyrefield had won the Prince of Wales's Plate at Punchestown he was sold to Germany for £1,000, a great price in those days. This sort of profitable dealing enabled Linde not only to improve his training facilities but also to invest in any and every horse his shrewd eye told him showed promise of success. The results, as will be seen, were to astonish the racing world.

Linde was among the first and was certainly the greatest of the early 'gentlemen' trainers. It is said, however, that the distinction of being the very first of those to whom the gentry sent their horses to be trained instead of keeping them at home under their own training-grooms falls to John Hubert Moore of Jockey Hall, the Curragh. Moore's earliest patron was Captain John Montgomery, commonly known as 'Rufus', a name which he also gave to one of his best horses. Rufus and many others were winners, and these successes, coinciding with the decline of the great estates and the fortunes of their owners brought about by the Land Acts, influenced many of the landed classes to avail themselves of Moore's services. The gentry soon came to realise that the professional approach of public trainers, combined with the improved facilities they could provide, gave their horses more chances of realising their potential than if they were trained at home. More and more, too, men of wealth from the cities, bankers, merchants and the like, who had no estates behind them were, with the spread of permanent 'enclosed' courses all over the country, coming into racing, and it was natural that these should seek the services of public trainers who could manage, school and enter their horses for them.

Both Moore and Linde had steeplechase courses for schooling laid out on their training grounds. Linde indeed, in addition to having a private 'park' course, had replicas of the Grand National fences, the Chair and Becher's and Valentine's Brooks, built for him and constantly schooled his Grand National entries over them.

Willie Moore.

Garrett Moore.

Both Moore and Linde had another inestimable advantage in that they could command the services of two distinct and immensely talented families of gentlemen riders. In the case of Moore these were his sons, Garrett and Willie, both of whom he had himself introduced to racing and whose skills he had carefully nurtured. Willie, after some successful seasons at home, did much of his racing on the continent, where he rode for the wealthy German sportsman Herr Otto Oehlschlager, for whom he won the Old Baden Hunt Steeple-chase, the chief amateur event in Germany, no less than four times in five years. Garrett divided his time between Ireland and England. In both countries he was soon near the top of the list of winning riders. In England, for instance, in the year 1871, despite the calls of his home stable, he tied for third place with the crack Mr J. M. Richardson, who won the Grand National twice in 1873 and 1874 on Disturbance and Reugny. The only riders to occupy a higher place in the list were Jack Goodwin and the champion jockey of 1871, Arthur Yates, who between the years 1869 and 1876 rode the astonishing total of 253 winners.

Garrett's greatest triumph was his victory on The Liberator in the Grand National in 1879. Well-named, for he was by Daniel O'Connell out of Mary O'Toole, The Liberator was a difficult horse both to train and ride — a 'cunning old devil', according to J. M. Richardson, who knew him well. It was probably for this reason that his owner, Mr Enoch, an auctioneer and dealer, who had bought him for £500 as a five-year-old, put him up for sale at his horse repository after he had fallen in the 1876 Grand National. He was knocked down to John Hubert Moore and Mr Plunkett Taaffe in equal shares of £500. The Liberator was third in the Grand National in the following year when ridden by the famous Tommy Pickernell; in 1878 he was taken out of the race at the last minute, a scratching which caused considerable controversy; and in 1879 there was further trouble arising from a disagreement between the joint owners. The cause of the dispute is obscure, but it may have had its origin in the circumstances surrounding the previous year's scratching. At all events, immediately before the race Mr Taaffe sought an injunction to prevent the horse from running. At almost the last moment the Master of the Rolls refused the application, but, possibly because of the litigation or a settlement out of court after it, the horse started in Garrett's name. He won easily from Lord Marcus Beresford's Jackal, and thus the ill-advised action of Mr Taaffe was the means by which Garrett Moore gained the honour of being only the second owner-rider to triumph in what was by then universally acknowledged as the blue riband of steeplechasing.

For Linde it was the Beasley brothers who performed the same services as Garrett and Willie Moore did for their father. But before chronicling the Linde and Beasley domination of the steeplechasing world which was to come about in the next decade and which was to earn for it its appellation as the 'golden age' of Irish steeplechasing it is necessary to return to the flat. For it was just before the period of Linde's greatest successes that the career of Barcaldine began. Through no fault of his own Barcaldine missed classic honours, and, like Harkaway, he may well have failed to realise his true potential because of misadventure and mishandling. His achievements, nonetheless, had the stamp of greatness upon them, and he triumphantly restored the prestige of Irish racing and breeding.

7

Barcaldine and Bendigo

1

As with his might predecessors Birdcatcher and Harkaway, there was much that was strange about both Barcaldine's begetting and his career.

Mr George Low, a hard-headed Scotsman, had left his native country about the middle of the century and settled at Burton, near Athy, Co. Kildare. There he bought up extensive tracts of land, farmed them and bred racehorses. One of his mares was Bon Accord, whom he had purchased from Mr Christopher St George of Tyrone House, Co. Galway, one of the many 'men of the west' who were so prominent in Irish racing at that time. Bon Accord was by Adventurer out of Darling's Dam, and in due course Mr Low sent her to be mated with Belladrum, a sire who had in his day been a leading two-year-old and winter favourite for the Derby. It was said of Belladrum during his two-year-old career that he 'could canter faster than most of them could gallop', but unfortunately before the classics were run in the following year he became a confirmed roarer. Although he did succeed in being second to Pretender in the Two Thousand Guineas of 1869, his affliction became rapidly worse. He was unplaced in the Derby, and Mr James Merry, the rich and ruthless Scottish ironmaster who owned him, quickly retired him to stud. But Mr Merry held him in the highest esteem as a racehorse. 'If Belladrum had only been the horse he was in 1868, no Pretender would have beaten him and no such horses as Perry Down and Martyrdom [third and fourth in the Two Thousand Guineas] would have got within sight of him,' he declared after the Derby, and these sentiments openly expressed may have played a part in Mr Low's decision to send Bon Accord to his fellow-countryman's stallion. If so, he was lucky enough to be able to secure his services, for Belladrum only stood for one season in England before Mr Merry, never one to refuse a profit, sold him to South Africa.

The mating in due course produced a filly whom Mr Low named Ballyroe after one of the townlands over which he farmed. Ballyroe ran four times as a two-year-old and failed to win. Deciding she was useless as a racehorse, Mr Low determined to breed from her. He must have thought something of her, for he chose Selim, Mr Cockin's Irish Derby winner of 1866, for her first covering, sending her the following year to Kingcraft, winner of the 1870 Epsom Derby. Finally she was mated to Solon, who when racing had carried the colours of Mr Christopher St George, the previous owner of Bon Accord. Solon was by West Australian, the 1853 Epsom Derby winner, out of Darling's Dam by Birdcatcher, and had been a useful though not outstanding racehorse. He had won races at two, three and four years, his victories including three Queen's Plates at the Curragh, the Dee Stakes at Chester and the Great Foal Stakes at Epsom. He was never aimed at the classics, and in his one venture into high-class handicap company, the Cesarewitch of 1865, he ran down the field.

The result of this mating was a bay colt foal with a faint star on his forehead and one white hind leg. Mr Low named him Barcaldine after his home town in Argyllshire. It will be seen from the above account that not only was Barcaldine closely inbred (his mating has been called incestuous by one Turf writer), but he was far from being born in the purple, neither sire nor dam being of much account as racehorses, although Solon had already got Arbitrator, winner of the Liverpool Autumn Cup and the Great Lancashire Handicap, for Mr C. J. Blake. But from his breeding the colt was unlikely to aspire to classic honours, and no classic entries, either Irish or English, were made for him.

Mr Low's horses were trained for him by Thomas Connolly of Curragh View, and in 1879 Barcaldine was duly sent to him. As the colt progressed in his work Connolly soon began to sense his high quality. Determined not to rush him, he did not produce Barcaldine on the racecourse until September of the following year.

Mr Low had also in training with Connolly a three-year-old filly out of Bon Accord called Berengaria who was something of a flyer and who won her last race at Galway in August with untroubled ease. Early in September Connolly arranged a trial between the two, setting Barcaldine to concede 9lb to the filly. Mr Low came over to witness this trial; when he saw the colt slam the filly he could scarcely believe his eyes, nor would he accept the truth of the weights said to be carried by the work-riders until he had himself seen them through Connolly's weighing scales. Barcaldine then proceeded to win the Railway Stakes, the National Produce Stakes, the Beresford Stakes and the Paget Stakes at distances ranging from six

Barcaldine.

furlongs to one mile, all very much as he liked. He finished his two-year-old season unbeaten — indeed it could be said that he had scarcely been challenged. He was ridden in all his races in Ireland by John Connolly, who, while being no relation to the trainer, was a nephew of the Patrick Connolly who has already been mentioned as the rider of Bran and Plenipotentiary in 1834.

2

George Low was a gambler both on and off the Turf. His horses, like Ferguson's, had to run for their keep and his pocket, and, like Ferguson, he took risks to see that they did. He was avaricious, and avarice was to prove his undoing and, tragically, to impair the career of his great horse. Having missed the chance of classic honours in 1881, he decided to run Barcaldine in two big English handicaps, the Manchester Cup and the Northumberland Plate. These appeared to him to be the best betting mediums for cashing in on Barcaldine's unquestioned promise and powers, for he had been assured by Connolly that the colt had wintered well. Both races were to be run in June, and Connolly aimed at giving Barcaldine time and producing him at his peak for them.

During the spring of 1881, however, something went seriously wrong with Mr Low's finances. Towards the end of April, therefore, he made the sudden decision to run Barcaldine in the Baldoyle Derby, for which he had been entered as a precaution and which was scheduled to take place a bare three weeks away. Despite Connolly's protests that the colt's preparation would now have to be rushed and that he could not possibly have him ready in time, Mr Low remained adamant that he must run.

Far from racing fit, carrying 9st 13lb and giving weight away all round, Barcaldine slammed a high-class field, defeating Theodora, a good filly of Garrett Moore's who was receiving 36lb, by a length.

This victory obviously held out high hopes for success in the Manchester Cup, but by now it seems that either his own greed or pressures from his creditors, or both, had Mr Low firmly in their grip. To the utter amazement of all concerned, especially that of his indignant trainer, when Mr Low saw the strength of the entries opposing his colt, which included Sir John Astley's Peter and Fred Archer's mount, Valour, and despite the attractive price of 25 to 1 offered about him, his nerve failed him and he struck Barcaldine out of the race. The reasoning behind this strange decision was based on Mr Low's hope that the good horses would exhaust themselves in the Cup and would in consequence be scratched from the Plate, thus making Barcaldine a racing certainty in it; furthermore, since he would not have run since Baldoyle, and since Irish form was in any event always suspect, it seemed certain that he would start at an attractive price. Mr Low was correct in thinking that the field for the Plate would cut up, but wrong in assuming that the price would be right, for when the ante-post market opened the defections were so many that Barcaldine was installed as favourite at 7 to 2 against.

No one knows just what happened next, and probably no one ever will. According to one version, Low sent a telegram to Sir John Astley, Peter's owner, a rumbustious character famous for his wit and known everywhere as 'the Mate', who also happened to be a member of the Jockey Club, offering to scratch Barcaldine from the Northumberland Plate in return for a payment of £1,000. Another, and perhaps more likely, account has it that this proposal was made to a leading bookmaker, who passed the letter on to Sir John, asking for action to be taken on it. Wherever the truth of the matter lies, it is clear that Mr Low held out an inducement to someone for the scratching of the favourite, that it was brought to the notice of a person in authority — probably Sir John Astley — and that he reported it to the Stewards of the Jockey Club. It is also a fact that, whether he received financial recompense or not, Mr Low did take Barcaldine out of the Northumberland Plate. Having done so, he then received a summons to appear before the Stewards of the Jockey Club at the Newmarket July Meeting to explain his conduct.

The peril of the position in which he stood must by then have been brought home to Barcaldine's owner. Desperate measures were needed if he were to do anything at all to recoup his finances; and, through Barcaldine, he speedily took them. At the Curragh June Meeting he started the colt on each of its three days. On the first, carrying 3lb overweight, he won His Majesty's Plate of two miles, and on the second, with 7lb overweight, a Queen's Plate of three miles. On the third day, fortunately for his constitution, his two previous victories had been so easily gained that the opposition was frightened off and he was given a walkover in another Queen's Plate of three miles. The Irish Derby was run on the second day of the meeting, and in it Master Ned, whom he had trounced as a two-year-old and in the Baldoyle Derby, ran out a convincing winner, demonstrating yet another proof of Barcaldine's prowess. A little over a fortnight later the Stewards of the Jockey Club sat on Mr Low's case and, after hearing the evidence, declared him a disqualified person and warned him off the Turf.

Barcaldine remained in Mr Low's ownership but could not, of course, run in his name. He was therefore absent for the remainder of the 1881 season. An effort was made to bring him back in 1882. There was a purported sale, and he was entered in the new owner's name for the Cesarewitch and the Cambridgeshire. Sent to Newmarket to be prepared for these big handicaps, he was ridden in a training gallop by Fred Archer, who, on dismounting, told his trainer he was useless. On Archer's advice he was taken out of the Cesarewitch in the hope of getting him fit enough to do himself justice in the Cambridgeshire.

But by this time, since the name of the purchaser had been given as 'a gentleman resident in the West Indies', suspicions had, not surprisingly, been aroused as to the authenticity of Barcaldine's purported sale. When the Cambridgeshire entries were closely examined it was found that the names and signatures were palpably false, and permission for him to run was refused. On the day after the race he was put up for auction, and Mr Tattersall knocked him down to Robert Peck, one of the great Victorian trainers, for 1,300 guineas.

Peck, who had won one Derby for Mr James Merry with Doncaster and another for the Duke of Westminster with Bend Or, ridden by his great friend Fred Archer, was then in semi-retirement, having his horses trained under his supervision by James Hopper, formerly his head lad, at Beverley House, Newmarket. Peck could gamble with the best of them, and he had collected a huge sum when his filly Hackness had won the Cambridgeshire on the previous day. It was the possession of this plunder from the bookmakers, combined with the fact that he was immediately attracted by Barcaldine's looks and divined the potential lurking in his great frame, that made him determined to buy the colt despite Archer's best efforts to prevent him. 'That hulking great Irish horse couldn't win a selling race,' Archer told him. In fact Archer, whose judgment was seldom at fault, was probably not wrong in this instance either, for, owing to his long lay-off, Barcaldine had completely lost his action, and it is likely that, even if he had been allowed to start in the Cambridgeshire, he would have been beaten.

The remainder of Barcaldine's career, since it took place in England, can only be briefly summarised.

Robert Peck gave him plenty of time to recover his action and come to hand, watching him fill out into what he had always promised to be — a magnificent specimen of the thoroughbred racehorse. Much later Joseph Osborne was to describe him as 'altogether as near perfection as a horse can be'. Peck produced him for the first time at Kempton in May 1883 in the Westminster Cup of 1¼ miles. The trainer made it clear that he did not believe the colt was yet ready to do himself justice, nor did he think that at the weights he was capable of beating the high-class field that opposed him. Gambler though he was, Peck did not have a shilling on him. To his astonishment Barcaldine easily disposed of his opponents, winning by a length from Tristan, the mount of Fred Archer. He was then sent to Epsom, where, ridden by Archer, he won the Epsom Stakes of 1½ miles. At Ascot he won the Orange Cup of three miles, while Tristan confirmed the form of the Kempton race by winning the Ascot Gold Cup. Peck then determined to win the Northumberland Plate with him, the race from which his scratching had brought about all his troubles two years before. Before this race Peck tried him a certainty by testing him against Hackness, the Cambridgeshire winner of the previous year: having given Hackness 56lb and a half-furlong start, Barcaldine left her standing.

But then, by a cruel stroke of fortune, his hopes of victory in the coming race seemed irretrievably doomed, for after that trial Barcaldine pulled out lame. He was consigned to walking exercise and to having his afflicted front leg stood in a bucket of water, which treatment continued up to and including the night before the race.

Yet Peck and Archer still believed in him. Their faith was justified, for, carrying 9st 10lb and conceding 17lb to the runner-up, he won at his ease.

Hurry On as a stallion.

Sadly, this proved to be Barcaldine's last race. When he was being prepared for the Cambridgeshire, for which he had been allotted the welter burden of 10st, the suspect tendon finally gave way. He broke down and was sold as a stallion to Lady Stamford for 8,000 guineas. On retiring to stud he carried with him the accolade of Robert Peck, whose flair as a judge of racehorses has seldom been bettered, that he was 'one of the greatest horses we have ever known', and Peck underlined that judgment by going on to say that he never knew how good he was. Fred Archer, too, handsomely withdrew his first hasty verdict and placed him among the four best horses he had ridden.

At stud Barcaldine did not perhaps quite achieve the success that had been hoped for him, though he was far from a failure, siring in all the winners of 212 races worth £77,658. Amongst his successful progeny were Mist, winner of the One Thousand Guineas and the Oaks in 1891, and Sir Visto, the Derby and St Leger victor of 1895, in which year Barcaldine stood second in the list of winning stallions. More important for posterity and for the future of the thoroughbred than these classic winners, gratifying though they were, was his siring of Marco out of Novitiate by Hermit. In 1895 from seven starts Marco won five races, including the Cambridgeshire under 7st 9lb and the Free Handicap. Marco got Marcovil, the winner of the Cambridgeshire in 1908, who in turn sired the unbeaten Hurry On, one of the most prepotent and successful stallions of all time. In addition, by covering Saltaich, a mare by St Simon, Marcovil got My Prince, who, when standing in Ireland between the wars, became pre-eminent as a sire of steeplechasers.

3

Before returning to steeplechasing in the 'golden age' of 1870-90 it is necessary to mention one other horse whose achievements on the flat brought distinction to his native land. Bendigo, by Ben Battle, winner of the Irish Derby in 1874, and out of Hasty Girl, was foaled two years after Barcaldine. Bred by Mr Moses Taylor, who lived near Newbridge, he was bought for £72 at the dispersal sale following Mr Taylor's death by the same Thomas Connolly who trained Barcaldine in his early days and who thus for a period had both these high-class colts in his yard at the same time.

Captain George Joy, an astute handler of bloodstock and spotter of talent, soon picked him out and negotiated his sale to Mr Hedworth Barclay for £1,000. 'Buck' Barclay, as he was familiarly known, was a distinguished gentleman rider and one of the best men across the country in Leicestershire. He sent him to be trained by Charles Jousiffe at Seven Barrows, Lambourn. For Mr Barclay he won the Lincolnshire Handicap, the first running of the Eclipse Stakes at Sandown in 1886, the Champion Stakes, the Jubilee Cup and that Cambridgeshire of 1883 which Barcaldine had had to miss through injury. Perhaps his greatest performance was in the Hardwicke Stakes of 1887, where he ran third to those two cracks of the day, classic horses in a vintage year, Minting and the mighty Ormonde. Giving them 2lb at weight-for-age, he was only beaten a head and three lengths, Ormonde just getting home from Minting after a desperate battle.

The great Mat Dawson, trainer of Minting and many classic winners, rated Bendigo in the very highest class of handicappers but not quite of winning classic standard. But Mr Barclay, who all but worshipped his horse, would have none of this. 'It always annoys me', he said, 'when I see in the papers that he was only a "handicap" horse and that when he met Ormonde and Minting at Ascot he was not in the same class. The horse was *absolutely* amiss that week. Upset by the noise of coach horns, etc., he was completely off his feed, so much so that I determined not to run him, and he was actually boxed and in the train ready to go home. But there was an accident on the line, and as there was no chance of getting home that day he was unboxed and brought back to the hotel stables. I feel certain that had be been *really* well and trained specially for the race he would have won it outright.'

A tremendously high-couraged horse, Bendigo inspired Adam Lindsay Gordon's lines: 'He cares not for the bubbles of fortune's fickle tide, Who like Bendigo can battle and like Oliver can ride.' He was eventually purchased by Count Woranzoff Dashkoff of the Russian Imperial Horse Breeding Board and ended his life standing in that country.

8

Linde and the 'Golden Age'

1

Henry Eyre Linde's domination of the steeplechasing scene began in earnest in 1880 when he won the Grand National with the mare Empress, named after the ill-fated Empress of Austria, who visited his stables with Captain 'Bay' Middleton during her hunting tour of Ireland in 1879. Linde won the race again the following year with Woodbrook, owned by Captain T. W. Kirkwood and named after his estate in the west of Ireland. Both these winners were ridden for him by Tommy Beasley, a member of the famous racing brotherhood whose feats have already been briefly mentioned and will now be dealt with in greater detail.

The four Beasley brothers came from a well-established Kildare family, their father being Joseph Lapham Beasley, who farmed three hundred acres near Athy and ranched a further thirty thousand acres of bog and moor, all of which had been inherited from his wife's grandfather, a Captain Lapham. Thomas, universally known as Tommy, was the eldest, the most successful and the most accomplished rider of the four. As we have seen, it was he who helped to set Linde on his path to success with his victories on Highland Mary at Fairyhouse and Punchestown while still in his teens. He was scarcely out of them when, in 1876, he rode the winners of the chief steeplechases in Ireland, the Irish Grand National, the Conyngham Cup and the Galway Plate, in the same year. In that Conyngham Cup he first showed his outstanding skill throughout a race and his strength in a finish. Riding Christmas Gift, he had a desperate struggle from the last fence with the vastly more experienced Garrett Moore on Scots Grey and just managed to get home by a neck. Tommy learnt the rudiments of his art under the great Allen McDonough, and Linde was quick to notice his promise and soon attached him to his stable. He was then, along with his three brothers, Harry, Johnny and Willie, accommodated in a house adjacent to the trainer's own. Once there, he was given the title of

Henry Eyre Linde.

manager, a purely honorary one in effect, for Linde allowed no one to interfere with the control of his string. It was conferred, so it was said, to preserve his somewhat precarious amateur status.

The quartet were of enormous assistance to Linde, and it may fairly be said that they constituted one of the corner-stones of his success. Apart from their prowess on the racecourse proper, all four were practical and polished schooling jockeys, Johnny and Willie having been taught their trade by John Hubert Moore, and Harry by Linde himself.

As jockeys the Beasleys dominated the Irish steeplechasing scene of that era every bit as much as their master Linde dominated it as a trainer. So consistently did Linde in these years sweep the board at Fairyhouse and Punchestown, especially the latter which was his home course, that Captain George Joy, the man who discovered Bendigo and many other good horses, christened him 'Farmer' Linde from his habit of 'farming' these races. On one occasion when congratulated by Lord Drogheda on a string of successes at Punchestown he replied: 'I am sorry, my lord, that Punchestown does not continue for a few days longer, for I have more horses to win more of your races.'

Some idea of the extent of the supremacy enjoyed by this confederacy may be given by recording that Tommy Beasley won the Irish Grand National in successive years 1876 (on the aptly named Grand National) and 1877 (on Thiggin Thue), the Conyngham Cup three times, the Aintree Grand National three times, and the Grand Steeplechase de Paris once. These were only the great races, without taking account of the countless victories in Ireland and England in minor events. Most, if not quite all, were on horses trained by Linde. 'Tom Oliver at his best could not give him 3lb over Aintree,' one good judge said of him. Astoundingly too, he was as good on the flat as over the fences and won the Irish Derby on three occasions.

Probably, however, the victory on the flat which gave him the greatest pleasure was that achieved in a welter race at the Curragh in 1886. Fred Archer had come to Ireland specially to ride Cambusmore for Lord Londonderry in the Lord Lieutenant's Plate. Cambusmore won, and Mr C. J. Blake asked Archer to ride his Isidore the following day. Archer put up 5lb overweight to do it and duly won, but in the last race of the day, the Welter Plate, riding Black Rose, again for Mr Blake, he was unexpectedly beaten into third place by Tommy Beasley on Spahi, owned by Mr John Gubbins and trained by Linde, the second place being occupied by Mr Cullen on Lord Chatham. Tommy Beasley and the ruffianly 'Mr Abington', who, whatever faults he may have had, was an outstanding amateur rider, are believed to be the only amateurs ever to have won a race with the great Fred Archer behind them.

Cullen, the rider of the runner-up to Spahi, was one of two talented brothers, both of them successful amateur riders and trainers, whose feats were overshadowed by the Beasleys. They were 'men of the west' but moved to the Curragh, where Willie trained at Rossmore Lodge and Fred at Rathbridge Cottage. In 1889 Willie interrupted the Beasley run of successes in the Conyngham Cup by winning it for Mr G. Jackson on Royal Meath, an entire horse who won the Grand Steeple at Auteuil in the following year. Willie also rode the winners of the Galway Plate in 1885, 1887 and 1896 and owned and trained Wales, winner of the Irish Derby in 1897.

Harry Beasley, who took more mounts in public than Tommy and was said to be the better on a difficult horse, won the Aintree Grand National once and was runner-up twice. He won no less than six Sefton Steeplechases at Liverpool, and the Conyngham Cup fell to him the same number of times, his last victory in this race being on his own horse Lively Lad in 1905.

In 1910 at the age of fifty-eight and after thirty-nine strenuous years in the saddle, he rode St Columba's, owned and trained by himself, in the Kildare Hunt Cup at Punchestown. A fall at the up-

Willie Beasley.

bank past the stands appeared to put him out of the race. But nothing ever stopped Harry Beasley. He remounted, caught up with the field and, riding a desperate finish, got up to win by a head from Vanity Fair, who had led from the last and appeared to have the race in hand.

Nor was that his last appearance at Punchestown. In 1923, at the age of seventy-one, he went out in the four-mile Maiden Plate on his own mare Pride of Arras — and won. The reception he received from the crowd outdid anything heard before or since at the historic meeting, and when he had weighed in he was carried shoulder-high to be presented to the Governor-General, Tim Healy.

He died at the age of eighty-seven at Eyrefield House, the Curragh, in October 1939, four years after riding his last race, a 'bumper' at Baldoyle in which he was unplaced on his own mare Mollie. To complete the astonishing record, which is likely to stand for ever,

75

it should be added that he won the Irish Grand National twice, the Grand Steeple at Auteuil twice, the Grand Hurdle once, and was runner-up in a close finish on another occasion.

Neither Johnny nor Willie enjoyed quite the success of their brothers, though Johnny rode the winners of the Conyngham Cup in 1877 and the Irish Grand National in 1878. Willie won the Conyngham Cup in 1891, but his career was tragically cut short by his death in 1892 from injuries received in a terrible fall at the big double at Punchestown when riding All's Well in the Kildare Hunt Plate.

2

Linde's triumphs in France with horses trained by him and ridden by Tommy and Harry Beasley deserve a further mention, as the Grand Steeple and the Grand Hurdle have always been notoriously difficult for foreign horses to win and were, of course, even more so a hundred years ago when it took four days to transport a racehorse from Ireland to France. In 1880 Harry was second on Turco in the Grand Hurdle and returned the next year to win it on Seaman. In 1882 and 1883 Linde won the Grand Steeple with Too Good and Whisper Low (the former named by the Empress of Austria, who, on seeing him schooled, exclaimed: 'Oh, this is too good!'), ridden respectively by Harry and Tommy. In fact in 1882 Linde almost brought off a unique double, for Mohican, ridden by Harry, was second in the Grand Hurdle. And in 1883 horses trained by Linde occupied two of the first three places in the Grand Steeple, for Mohican, again ridden by Harry, was third to Whisper Low. To win the Grand Steeple twice and the Grand Hurdle once and provide two runners-up and a third, all in the space of four years, is a feat of training and riding in these races never equalled before or since by trainers or riders from Great Britain or Ireland.

Seaman, the winner of the Grand Hurdle in 1881, was in the following year to be the instrument of one of Linde's rare misjudgments and a defeat when the money was down, something more than unusual in his brilliantly successful career.

Seaman was bred by Captain Stamer Gubbins by his own sire Xenophon out of Lena Rivers. A wretched-looking yearling, he was not considered worth putting into the sale of Captain Gubbins's bloodstock which took place after his death. But Linde spotted him and bought him cheaply in a private deal, as indeed he did with many of his good horses (Lord Tara and Gamebird, for instance, prolific winners both, cost him only £5 and £65 respectively). Seaman never grew beyond 15.3 hands, and throughout his career he was dreadfully unsound – he was fired on both his hocks before he ever saw a racecourse – but he soon showed Linde that he could gallop and

jump. In 1881 as a five-year-old he carried 11st 7lb and Harry *Lord Manners on Seaman.*
Beasley to victory in the Conyngham Cup, giving such a display of
fast, spectacular jumping over the banks as had seldom before been
seen. It was recorded of him that in this race he all but cleared the
big double, hitting the far side with one leg and landing a yard
beyond the ditch below it. In that year too he won the Liverpool
Hunt Steeplechase and, as has been said, the Grand Hurdle at
Auteuil, all of which victories represented no mean feat of training
by Linde of a thoroughly unsound horse.

After the Auteuil race, however, Seaman's legs were in a deplorable state. Harry Sargent picturesquely described them as being 'scarified with the irons from knees to knuckles and hocks to heels'. Linde decided that he would no longer stand training, and he was delighted when Captain James Machell came along and offered him £2,000 for the horse on behalf of a client of his, Lord Manners, the Master of the Quorn Foxhounds.

Lord Manners was a polished horseman and a brilliant man to hounds, but he had little experience of race-riding, though his name does appear in the *Racing Calendar* as having won the Lightweight Race at Rugby on his own horse Grenadier in 1880. However, having bought Seaman, he put both himself and the horse into the hands of Captain Machell and his trainer Jewett, than whom there were few better qualified to educate both horse and man, and some three weeks before the 1882 Grand National he won the Grand Military at Sandown on another horse of his own, Lord Chancellor.

Somehow Machell brought Seaman sound to the start at Aintree, though he made no secret of the fact that he had not been able to give him anything like a thorough preparation and that he was, to use his own words, 'only three parts trained'.

Linde totally discounted Seaman's chances. He had two runners in the race, Cyrus, ridden by Tommy Beasley, and Mohican, ridden by Harry, and he fancied them both. Mohican started favourite at 100 to 30, with Cyrus second favourite in the betting at 9 to 2.

The race was run in a blinding snowstorm. This ensured that there was give in the ground and that the pace would be slow. Lord Manners was therefore able to ride as if in a hunt, and all these factors may have assisted Seaman's chances. Mohican fell, and Cyrus and Seaman jumped the last together. With the leading rider pitted against an inexperienced amateur, all the way up that long run-in it looked a certainty for another triumph for the Linde stable, especially as on landing Manners had felt one of Seaman's suspect legs go. Seaman, however, had already shown himself to be a horse of tremendous class and courage. In the soft ground he ran on gamely, and Manners had the sense to sit still. Although the Irish contingent were already roaring Cyrus home, Seaman snatched a tenuous lead and, despite everything Tommy Beasley could do, held on to win by a short head.

But such misjudgments and setbacks were rare indeed in Linde's career. A hard taskmaster both of horses and men and a perfectionist in all he did, he was rough-tongued, ready-witted and no respecter of persons or pomposity. A grandiloquent foreigner who once tried to impress him with his lineage by saying that his father was a baron was crushed by the instant retort 'A pity your mother wasn't barren too.'

The defeat of Cyrus by Seaman ended for the time being the Irish run of successes in the Grand National until they were restored by Tommy Beasley on Frigate in 1889. Frigate was owned and trained by Matthew A. Maher of Ballinkeele, Co. Wexford, a Steward of the INHSC and a member of the Turf Club. Maher came from an old Tipperary family whose association with horses, hunting and racing stretched back over many years. His older cousin, Valentine Maher, had, in the days of the Regency bucks, spent his hunting season at Melton Mowbray, where he had been rated as the best man to hounds with the shire packs, superior even to such cracks as 'Squire' Osbaldeston and the Marquis of Waterford. Moving to Wexford and purchasing an estate at Ballymurn in that county, Maher built a mansion and extensive stabling, and it was there that he trained Frigate and many other good horses.

At first, so far as the Grand National was concerned, Frigate seemed fated to be unlucky. Always ridden by one or other of the Beasley brothers, she was second in 1884, 1885 and 1888. In between achieving the latter two second places Maher had parted with her, and shortly afterwards she changed hands for a second time. Indifferently ridden in the Nationals of 1886 and 1887, she fell in the first and was pulled up in the second. Mr Maher then bought her back. She was unlucky again in 1888, when, ridden this time by Willie Beasley, she was all but knocked over by his brother Harry on the Linde-trained Usna at the Canal Turn but ran on gamely to finish second.

Although there was some stable confidence behind her when Tommy Beasley went out on her for the National of 1889, there was also trepidation that her jinx might be still pursuing her. This was increased on the day of the race, when she was seen to be 'taking a walk in the market', with her odds steadily lengthening before the off. She had been backed heavily both on and off the course by her connections, some of whom remained in England awaiting the result. They stayed on tenterhooks until news of her victory came through, George Silke, the stable commissioner, wiring them: 'Man, mare and money all right.'

In that same year, 1889, Harry Beasley won the Irish Grand National on his own horse Citadel; and, as if winning at Aintree for the third time had not been sufficient triumph for Tommy, he went on to win the Irish Derby on Captain Harry Greer's filly Tragedy. For an amateur to win both of these events in the same year is a record which has never been equalled, nor is it likely to be. For good measure Tommy also won the Cork Derby that year on Tragedy.

Captain Harry Greer.

4

Tragedy was the first racehorse to carry the colours of Captain Harry Greer, then a young man about to resign his commission in the Highland Light Infantry and devote his whole life to racing and breeding. With this in mind he purchased Brownstown House, the Curragh, for his future stud and looked about for a stallion to install there. His choice fell on one who was to stamp his name and fame on future generations of the Irish thoroughbred, for in 1889 he purchased Gallinule from the dissolute George Alexander Baird, who raced under the *nom de course* of 'Mr Abington' and was known universally to the fancy and others as 'the Squire'.

Foaled in 1884, Gallinule, by Isonomy out of Moorhen by Hermit, was sold on the death of his breeder, Mr J. C. Hill, in 1886 to Lord Savernake, a fellow-roisterer of the Squire's who went by the name of 'Billy Stomachache'. As a two-year-old Gallinule proved promising enough for his new owner, winning three races to the value of £1,985. Then, just as his maternal grandfather Hermit had done, he started breaking blood-vessels. His three-year-old career was a disaster for all concerned. Not only did he fail to win, but so suspicious were the circumstances surrounding his running in the Great Yorkshire Stakes that the matter was referred to the Stewards of the Jockey Club. These gentlemen, who had not looked on Billy Stomachache with any great favour before, promptly warned him off the Turf.

Gallinule was put up for auction and was bought by Baird for the handsome sum of £5,000, his owner having omitted to advise his friend of his infirmity. Running for Baird, he proved even a worse failure than he had been for Billy Stomachache, for it was discovered that in addition to being a bleeder he had also gone in the wind. Anxious to be rid of his bad bargain, Baird first offered him to the sporting writer Charles Richardson for £1,000. When this offer was refused Baird instructed Morton, his trainer, to find a buyer somewhere. Hearing that he was on the market and having conceived a linking for the Isonomy blood, Greer entered into negotiations with Morton for his purchase. Aided by a friendly and foolish veterinary surgeon who passed him sound and who cannot have realised the service he was rendering Greer by so doing, a deal was made for £900. When told of this by Morton, Baird, delighted to be rid of him, announced at the top of his voice in his uninhibited way: 'No one but a mad bloody Irishman would have bought that horse.' Time was to prove how wrong he was.

Mated with Greer's good mare Tragedy, Gallinule first got Wildflower, winner of the St Leger in 1898, and, subsequently, Slieve Gallion, winner of the Two Thousand Guineas in 1907. Amongst a host of other winners he sired the winner of every Irish Derby except one between the years 1895 and 1901. In 1904 he headed the list of winning stallions. His most famous offspring was Major Eustace Loder's immortal mare Pretty Polly. Altogether for 'the mad bloody Irishman' he proved himself one of the most prepotent and successful sires ever to stand in Ireland. His owner too was to have a long and distinguished career on the Turf: he eventually became the first director of the National Stud and was later knighted for his services to racing.

The year 1891, the first of Gallinule's covering seasons at Brownstown, when even Captain Greer, it seems, had some doubts as to the wisdom of his purchase — for he offered his services free to approved mares — also saw Mat Maher back again in an important winner's enclosure. This time it was at the Curragh, having won the Irish Derby with his colt Kentish Fire, a close relation to his beloved Frigate. Kentish Fire was ridden by Michael Dawson, who during the next thirty years was to carve out for himself one of the most successful riding and training careers in the history of the Irish Turf.

5

In 1892 Tommy Beasley scored a second success in the Irish Derby, this time on Narragh, trained in England by Charles Archer, the tragic Fred's younger brother. But public attention was focused less on the Curragh than on some controversial events that had taken place on Ireland's newest racecourse, Leopardstown. At the Leopardstown June Meeting there had occurred an extraordinary series of objections, none of which were determined by the local stewards and all of which were referred to the Senior Stewards of the Turf Club, who took their time deliberating upon them. This delay, necessitating the suspension of the settlement of all bets, caused a volley of furious criticism to be launched by press and public at the Leopardstown management. Leopardstown was no stranger to such attacks, for the new course had experienced stormy birth-throes.

Leopardstown racecourse owed its existence to the enterprise and initiative of an Englishman, Captain George Quin, and was inspired by the success of Sandown Park, of which it was an avowed imitation. While on a visit to Ireland Quin had noted the similarity of the site facing the railway to that of Sandown. He bought up the land cheaply and then formed a syndicate to exploit it as a race-course. This syndicate was formed from its founder's English friends, and the original capital of the company was only £20,000. Once the preliminaries had been settled, work went ahead rapidly. The stands and amenities were an exact copy of those at Sandown and were, just as at the Esher course, situated on the slope facing the railway, a layout subsequently criticised on the grounds that it deprived the public of a view of the Dublin mountains. One difference between the two courses was, however, that Leopardstown was a left-handed track, while at Sandown the opposite was the case.

Before the opening meeting on 27 August 1888 there was a tremendous publicity build-up. Advertisements were splashed across the leading daily and provincial papers, the proximity to Dublin and easy access by road and rail being stressed, as was the fact that the chief race was to be an Inaugural Gold Cup. Special trains were organised to run from Harcourt Street station. When the day arrived the weather smiled. It was a beautiful balmy August afternoon. All seemed set for success.

Unfortunately the promoters were caught in a trap of their own devising and found themselves utterly unprepared for the success of their advertising and pre-race ballyhoo. Enormous crowds had assembled, and the executive could in no way cope with them. Everything broke down. Racecards ran out early, but that was only the beginning. Restaurant facilities proved hopelessly inadequate, and no proper arrangements had been made to control the press of traffic on the roads, which quickly became chaotic. The special trains laid on were insufficient to carry the throng of eager racegoers anxious to sample the spectacle of high-class racehorses competing against each other almost on their doorstep and to try out the vaunted modern stands and other amenities offered by the advertisements. Many never reached the racecourse at all; near riots occurred on some stations; the turnstiles were crammed and could not cope with the press of people; some were even trampled underfoot. Altogether it was not surprising that one sporting paper published the following squib:

Sacred
to the memory of
LEOPARDSTOWN
foully and brutally
strangled at birth
by gross incompetence
bungling and mismanagement
August 27 1888

Undaunted, however, by these teething troubles, Captain Quin and his team pressed on. They were enterprising and forward-looking and soon were to stage a Leopardstown Grand Prize of £1,000, the first race to be run for such a large sum of money in Ireland. The stewarding trouble of 1892 was only a minor setback, for trainers and owners were quick to recognise the worth of the new galloping course and gladly patronised it. The public too, attracted by the setting, the standard of sport provided and its proximity to the city, soon forgot their early discomforts and returned to popularise it.

Once again that year Linde, who had been one of the first to support Leopardstown, was champion trainer, as he was to be for the next three years also. But his health was beginning to fail. The next year, 1893, was the last time he had a runner placed in the Irish Derby. First Flower, owned and trained by him, was second to his old friend and rival Mat Maher's Bowline, who carried Michael Dawson to his and Maher's second victory in Ireland's premier classic. Neither was Linde quite the force in steeplechasing that he had been in previous years, nor were horses owned, trained and ridden by Irishmen so dominant at Aintree as they once were,

though in 1891 Comeaway, the mount of Harry Beasley, beat the mighty Cloister, ridden by that prince of soldier riders, Captain Roddy Owen, in a controversial finish.

Comeaway just led Cloister over the last, and on the long run-in Owen constantly tried to get up on Beasley's inside. The Irishman was far too experienced to have anything to do with that. He closed the gap. One racing journalist described the position of the two horses and riders: 'Harry had the Captain in the same position as a man with a cork halfway in the neck of a bottle, one little push and it will go down.' Beasley won by half a length, and Owen objected. A mob of furious Irishmen, who were on Beasley to a man, all but stormed the weighing-room, threatening to lynch the objector. Roddy Owen, who feared nothing and had never been known to yield an inch to anyone, either on horse or on foot, faced them saying: 'All right, but wait till it's settled, then I will fight any one of you singlehanded or the whole lot of you together.' When it *was*

84

settled the objection was overruled, tempers calmed, and with the Irish contingent recognising coolness and courage when they saw it, no lives were lost.

Owen came into his own next year when he took the mount on Father O'Flynn and, receiving 30lb, beat his former mount, Cloister. In the following year, 1893, after running second twice, Cloister proved himeself one of the greatest of all Grand National winners, winning by forty lengths carrying 12st 7lb, the first horse ever to win under that huge burden. Cloister had been bred in Ireland and had won his early races there, but on the occasion of his victory he was English owned, trained and ridden. Father O'Flynn, oddly enough, considering his name, had no Irish connections, being bred in Shropshire, ridden by a Welshman, and owned and trained in England.

There was no runner from the Linde stable in that National. The onslaught of Bright's disease forced his retirement in 1895. The Marquis of Drogheda too had by then gone from the racing scene, for he had died suddenly in London, at the age of sixty-six, from a heart attack on 29 June 1892, and very soon there was a new hand on the reins of power.

9

C. J. Blake, John Gubbins and F. F. MacCabe

1

It was Mr C. J. Blake of Heath House, Maryborough, who stepped into the shoes vacated by Lord Drogheda. Already for years he had been the Marquis's right-hand man. Now he was to exercise authority with firmness and fairness for the next thirty years. No one could accuse him of lack of enthusiasm or support for the Turf, for before his accession to the seat of power he had twice been the leading owner in Ireland.

Although qualified as a barrister, Mr Blake never practised, his entire life being devoted to racing and the Turf. For many years his learning in the law had, however, been constantly called upon by his fellow-stewards when problems arose as to the interpretation of rules and articles and the settling of disputes. His knowledge of racing was every bit as profound as that of his predecessor, but his opinions were more fixed and his mind less open to argument or persuasion. A contemporary wrote of him: 'There is no man in the Irish Turf Club or outside it who has such a complete grasp of the complicated code of Irish racing as Mr C. J. Blake. He is slow to make up his mind on any subject that comes before the Club in a judicial capacity or otherwise, so once he comes to a conclusion it is not easy to change it.'

He was quiet and reserved in manner, detesting all sham or show, and any attempt to influence a decision or prejudge an issue, no matter from what quarter it came, received scant attention from him. A revealing anecdote is told of him concerning an occasion when he had to adjudicate on an objection arising out of a very rough race at the Curragh. The owner who made the objection informed the stewards in a blustering manner that if the jockey he had picked out as the offender was not warned off he himself would never race in Ireland again. The evidence as given was not sufficient, in Mr Blake's opinion, to sustain the objection, nor did

C. J. Blake.

it point to the jockey in question as being the originator of the trouble or the sole offender. Accordingly the objection was over-ruled, and no action was taken against the jockey. When he had given the decision Mr Blake turned to the owner who had made the pronouncement and said to him in his quiet and commanding way: 'I do not think, sir, that it will make any great difference to the fortunes of the Irish Turf whether you race on it again or not.'

2

John Gubbins, brother of Captain Stamer Gubbins, whose stud farms at Knockany and Bruree he had inherited, was also coming to the fore as an owner on a princely scale. His first Irish Derby winner was Blairfinde in 1894, but before that he had headed the list of winning owners on three occasions. A great sportsman on every count and a cross-country rider himself until increasing weight made him hang up his boots, he had won the Downshire Plate at Punchestown back in 1870 carrying 13st 8lb, and had been second in the following year, beating his friend Linde, who trained his steeplechasers for him, into third place. Thirteen years later he won the Welter Cup at Down Royal on his own horse DPS, weighing out with the astonishing burden of 15st 8lb; then, with a pound less to carry, he went to Cork Park with the same horse and won again. Since the runners-up in these two races were, respectively, Garrett Moore and Captain Kirkwood, the latter's mount being Blackbird, owned and trained by Linde, it will be seen that he had something to beat. Still later he and Linde rode a private match over Linde's schooling ground for 100 guineas a side, both of them carrying catch-weights of over 16st. They collided at the third fence, and both came down. One of the stable-lads standing by caught Gubbins's horse and decamped with it to the stable-yard, leaving his master to win as he liked. The stakes, it is said, were celebrated in whiskey and champagne.

Gubbins was also Master of the Limerick Foxhounds from 1880 to 1886 and started his own pack of staghounds there which he kennelled at Bruree. But this was the time when the Land League was at its most active, and hunting, possibly because the red coats of the hunt staffs called to mind the military uniforms of the hated oppressor, was one of the main objects of its antipathy and harassment. The League's activities made it impossible for Gubbins to pursue his sport, the final insult coming when his hounds were set upon by a gang who attacked them with staves and threw rocks and stones at them. 'For God's sake, leave the hounds alone; I'd rather you threw your stones at me,' Gubbins shouted. With the aid of his whippers-in he gathered his pack together, took them home and hunted no more. Immediately afterwards he transferred his racing interests to England, where his horses were trained for him first by G. W. Lushington and then by Sam Darling at Beckhampton; it was Darling who trained Blairfinde. Despite the treatment he had received, Gubbins retained his stud farms, spending much of his time upon them, and never lost his Irish interests or connections.

Sam Darling also trained for Captain Greer and was in partnership with him in many of his stud ventures. Tragedy was sent to him after she had won the Irish Derby, but she did not train on. After she had

John Gubbins.

produced Wildflower, with whom, as has been said, Darling won the
St Leger for her owner, she was sold by the partnership to Sir Tatton
Sykes for £5,000. It was with Captain Greer that Darling was staying
when he won the Irish Derby for John Gubbins with Blairfinde.
Linde and Darling were on terms of close friendship, their natural
rivalry being mingled with a deep respect for each other's talents.

Blairfinde started joint favourite with the Gallinule colt Baldcoote, owned and trained by Linde. Anxious to ascertain the strength of Darling's hand, Linde made a point of watching Blairfinde work on the morning of the race. Having done so, he remarked to Lord Enniskillen, a member of Greer's house party: 'I've just seen Sam Darling's horse and call him a damned coach-horse, and if he wins our Irish Derby I'll eat him!' When Blairfinde did win easily, with Baldcoote well down the field, Darling asked Linde when he proposed to begin his meal and whether he preferred his horseflesh roasted or grilled. Linde ruefully congratulated his friend saying: 'Old Jack Gubbins might have told me his horse was going to win, especially as I was staying with him.' In fact Darling had tried to buy Baldcoote from Linde as a yearling, but the price, 100 guineas, was too high for him, so that Derby victory was doubly gratifying.

Blairfinde was by Kendal out of Morganette, a mare by Springfield out of Lady Morgan by Thormanby out of Morgan la Faye. Gubbins could never remember the exact price he paid for the mare, but he put it in the region of £200 or £300. She proved to be the best investment he ever made, and one of the greatest bargains in the history of Irish thoroughbred. In 1894 she produced at Bruree a big bay colt foal, a full brother to Blairfinde, whose commanding presence so impressed Gubbins that he named him Galtee More after the highest peak of the mountain range overlooking his stud.

In due course Galtee More was sent to Sam Darling, and he was not slow in demonstrating both his quality and classic prospects. On his first appearance he won the Hurstborne Stakes at Stockbridge with an ease and authority which convinced Darling that here he had indeed something special. In all, during his two-year-old career he was only beaten once in five starts, his most impressive victory being in the Middle Park Plate, run in what Darling considered to be the worst going ever experienced at Newmarket.

Galtee More's three-year-old career was one of unqualified triumph. He won the Two Thousand Guineas, the Derby and the St Leger virtually unchallenged, becoming the first Irish-bred and Irish-owned colt to win the Derby and sweep the board in the three classics, thus gaining the coveted if mythical Triple Crown. In addition to his classic victories, he won the Newmarket Stakes, the Prince of Wales Stakes at Ascot, the Sandringham Cup and the Sandown Foal Stakes at Sandown. In the Cambridgeshire, saddled with the crippling burden of 9st 6lb, he suffered his only defeat of the year finishing fifth in a very close-run race in which, despite his position, he was within a length of the winner, Comfrey, to whom he was giving no less than 2st 4lb. Edward Moorhouse, by far the most knowledgeable and reliable of all Derby historians, rated him 'a veritable Triton among minnows', holding that none of his contemporaries was within 10lb of him. He went on to say that the only credit accruing from his performances that England could claim

was that he was trained by Sam Darling. Commenting further on his victory, Moorhouse declared: 'No phase in the history of the British thoroughbred is more interesting or more significant than that which concerns the developments that have taken place in Ireland. As a breeding centre the Emerald Isle has during the past quarter of a century acquired a world-wide fame.' Galtee More also put Gubbins top of the list of winning owners in England, the first Irishman to occupy that position.

Although Darling had hoped to train Galtee More for the Cup races in the following year, he knew he had a suspect leg which made it doubtful if it would stand up to racing. When, therefore, the Russian Imperial Horse Breeding Board offered Mr Gubbins £20,000 for the colt he could not find it in him to oppose the sale. Galtee More was accordingly exported and proved a successful sire in his new country. For some unknown reason, after six seasons the Russians sold him to Germany for a sum said to be £14,000. He died there during the First World War.

Galtee More, C. Wood up.

All in all, the year 1897 was an epic and eventful one in Irish racing, for it also saw Leopardstown playing host to royalty in the persons of the Duke and Duchess of York, later to become King George V and Queen Mary. It was in this year too that there occurred, almost inevitably, it seemed at the time, yet another Leopardstown sensation, though this one was more serious than most.

The royal visit itself, which took place at the second summer meeting of 21 and 23 August, passed off successfully and without incident. Accompanied by the Lord Lieutenant, Lord Cadogan, himself an owner and a racing man, the Duke and Duchess expressed themselves delighted with the amenities and the entertainment. There were no demonstrations or expressions of protest or ill-will towards the royal visitors, but behind the scenes something was happening of grave concern to the racing itself and its future on the course.

Captain George Quin had remained in sole and undisputed command of Leopardstown's fortunes since its inception. An authoritarian by nature, he was a law unto himself in all he did. Being cramped for room on the initial laying out of the track, he had designed a round five-furlong course. Its distance was accurate enough, but it was so much on the bend that owners and trainers disliked it and would not run their charges on it. After many complaints and subsequent falling off in the number of entries and runners Quin was obliged to install a straight five furlongs. This he did — or rather purported to do, for he was still short of space. Never being one, however, to concern himself with the niceties of a situation, and being well aware that at that time there was no official measuring of courses, Quin simply put down a start and finish, called it a straight five furlongs, and that — for the moment — was that.

But the results on the new track were from the first bewildering and continued to be so. No one could understand the returns of winners and placed horses when compared with those from elsewhere, and the handicapper continually complained that he 'could make neither head nor tail of the form on the Leopardstown five-furlong course'. No official action was, however, taken to investigate these extraordinary divergences of form until matters came to a head at that August Meeting.

F. F. MacCabe, who trained a small string of horses, mostly his own, at Sandyford, owned a filly, Sabine Queen, whom he strongly fancied for the two-year-old five-furlong Londonderry Plate. He had tried her over five furlongs at home, and timed her too, for he was a man of ideas in advance of his time. He was also a man of parts, for in addition to training horses he was a journalist, a qualified doctor, a racing cyclist and a cross-country runner. It was his exper-

P. P. Gilpin.

ience in athletics which gave rise to his theories of training by time He timed this particular trial at 66½ seconds.

Peter Purcell Gilpin also had a fancied runner, a filly called Medine, in the race. Gilpin, who was later to make a great name for himself in English racing, came from an old Kildare family. The family home was at Halverston, and his paternal grandfather had been the founder of the Royal Irish Agricultural Society. He himself had been born at Pau, the sporting centre in the foothills of the Pyrenees, and had been a serving soldier in the 5th Royal Irish Lancers until his wife inherited money, whereupon he sent in his papers and thereafter devoted himself to his lifelong passion for training racehorses.

MacCabe knew that Medine was fancied, and he knew too that Gilpin was both more experienced as a trainer than he was and had a better trial tackle in his stable with which to assess his filly's chances. Nevertheless he expected his own filly, Sabine Queen, if not to beat Medine, at least to give a good account of herself and finish close up to her. In the event Medine won handsomely, with Sabine Queen a well-beaten sixth. On coming in her jockey told MacCabe that the filly had been taken off her legs and that he had never had a chance to settle her.

MacCabe had already had his suspicions as to the accuracy of the advertised distance, and he had, as was his practice, timed the race. When he saw the result he could scarcely believe his eyes, for the stop-watch showed the time to be 56 seconds, a difference of 10½ seconds over five furlongs from that of his trial — which was incredible. MacCabe's suspicions now heightened into something approaching certainty, and he got hold of 'an engineer with a range-finder' to measure the course. The engineer's report showed that, as MacCabe had surmised, the distance was nothing like what it should have been, but was in fact something less than 4½ furlongs. Immediately MacCabe asked the Stewards of the Turf Club to declare the race void. His request was refused on the grounds that it constituted an objection and, as such, was out of time. This was a decision which the Stewards were, at least technically, quite entitled to arrive at, but it infuriated MacCabe. Forthwith he issued a challenge to Gilpin for a return match to be run at Baldoyle over the proper distance for stakes of £100 a side. Gilpin sportingly agreed to this, and a date was fixed.

Never averse to publicity, MacCabe astutely promoted the match, which, owing to the circumstances surrounding its inception, attracted great interest not only amongst racing men but also amongst the general public. Crowds flocked to Baldoyle to witness it, and MacCabe was handsomely vindicated when Sabine Queen, ridden by Michael Dawson, won with some ease. She was a useful filly, for she went on to win the Irish Oaks in the following year.

As for Quin, he was fined £100 by the Stewards and had, of course, to close the track. He constructed a new one on which, according to MacCabe, it was impossible from the stands to see either the start or the finish, and it was not until several years later that the Leopardstown executive were able to purchase land from 'Boss' Croker for £10,000 to enable them to lay out a satisfactory straight five furlongs.

There was sadness too in 1897, for on 18 March Linde died, worn out by the ravages of Bright's disease. His two marriages

Robert J. Goff.

had been childless, and a year after his death Eyrefield Lodge was sold by public auction, being knocked down to Captain Eustace Loder for £8,500, the under-bidder being R. C. Dawson. By a strange coincidence, after an enormously successful career on the Turf which earned him the sobriquet of 'Lucky' Loder, he too was to die of the same disease.

The auctioneer of Eyrefield Lodge was Robert J. Goff. As far back as 1866 Goff had been appointed official auctioneer to the Turf Club, the following announcement appearing in the *Irish Racing Calendar*:

95

Mr Robert J. Goff, Auctioneer, etc., Newbridge, County of Kildare (partner for several years with the late Mr Johnston), begs to announce that he has had the distinguished honour of being specially appointed

AUCTIONEER TO THE TURF CLUB.

Mr R. J. Goff respectfully informs Noblemen and Gentlemen that he will attend any Race Meetings, receiving due notice, to dispose of Winners of Selling Stakes, or conduct Sales of Blood-stock, and from his knowledge and experience of this branch of the business he trusts to give entire satisfaction and to merit a continuance of the patronage he may receive.

Thirty-one years after this announcement Mr Goff conducted his first sale of yearlings at his newly established sales paddocks at Ballsbridge, the initial lot into the ring being, appropriately enough, a brown filly by Mr C. J. Blake's stallion Arbitrator, which was sold for 350 guineas.

4

In steeplechasing too 1897 was a memorable year for Ireland, for the great Manifesto, claimed by some to be the best of all Grand National winners up to the time of the changing of the fences in 1961 (since when no comparison is possible), won the race for the first time. He was to repeat his victory two years later under 12st 7lb, but by that time he had passed out of Irish ownership. Manifesto was bred by his owner Mr Harry Dyas in 1888 on his farm near Navan. He was a truly Irish-bred horse, for he was by Man of War by Ben Battle (Bendigo's sire) by Rataplan, out of Vae Victis by King Victor.

Manifesto's racing career commenced as a four-year-old when he won the Irish Champion Steeplechase at Leopardstown. The rest of his racing was done in England, and when he achieved his great victory in 1897 he was trained for Mr Dyas by William McAuliffe at Everleigh in England, but he was ridden by an Irishman, Terry Kavanagh, who had learnt his trade with Linde. So, as with Galtee More in the same year, it can be said that the only credit accruing to England for his victory was that he happened to be trained there.

Early in the following year Mr Dyas sold Manifesto to Mr J. G. Bulteel, father of the late Sir John Crocker Bulteel, Clerk of the Course at Ascot for many years. The price was £4,000, but for some reason which has never been accurately ascertained he did not compete in the Grand National of that year. However, he was back again next time to win, as has been said, under 12st 7lb. There was an Irish flavour, if no more, to this victory, for although the records give the trainer's name as Collins, the man responsible was in fact Willie Moore, son of John Hubert Moore and brother of Garrett, for whom Collins held the licence.

The rest of Manifesto's career at Liverpool can be briefly summarised: he was third in 1900, 1902 and 1903, carrying the crippling weights of 12st 13lb, 12st 8lb and 12st 5lb; in 1904, at the age of sixteen, he was sixth with 12st 4lb on his back. Altogether it is not surprising that Emil Adam, the famous German painter of racehorses, expressed astonished admiration when he came to paint him. Accustomed to commissions from crowned heads, and to having only those horses bred in the purple paraded before him, he had accepted with reluctance the task of painting a 'mere steeplechaser'. But immediately he laid eyes on Manifesto he exclaimed aloud: '*Mein Gott!* Vy, zizz is a racehorse!'

Manifesto's victory in 1899 was in fact the second Grand National triumph for Moore and Collins since they had also won the race in 1896 with The Soarer, an Irish-bred horse by Skylark out of Idalia, a mare who had herself won steeplechases and who traced back to Uncas and Sir Hercules. David Campbell, then a subaltern in the 9th Lancers quartered in Ireland, spotted him as an unbroken four-year-old in a field belonging to his breeder, Mr Pat Doyle, and bought him for a small sum. His first race was the Irish Grand Military, in which, ridden by his owner, he finished second. In the following year Campbell put him in the care of Willie Moore and Collins at Weyhill. Dedicating himself to the task of winning the great race with him, he rode him in all his work and all his races. The Soarer's performance, however, was somewhat disappointing, for he won only one race out of eleven starts before going to Liverpool. Perhaps for that reason Campbell, although he retained the ride, sold him for £500 to the eccentric sportsman Mr William Hall-Walker, later to gain the rank of colonel, to be elected MP for the Widnes division of Lancashire and still later to be elevated to the peerage under the title of Lord Wavertree.

Hall-Walker had ridden with some success under pony club rules, his extensive business interests preventing him from being other than a 'weekend' competitor. He was always fascinated by breeding and its theories, upon which he was later to put forward some distinctly original propositions based on astrology, and it is perhaps not surprising that after his Grand National victory his attentions and ambitions should turn towards the flat. In 1900 he purchased a thousand acres of some of the best land in Kildare and there set up the Tully Stud, where he bred on an extensive scale and raced his own produce. His first year, 1901, showed only a return of £770 in stakes, but thereafter, as will be seen, he was increasingly successful and was soon elected a member of the Irish Turf Club.

10

Fin de Siècle

1

Before The Soarer's win in 1896 and between Manifesto's triumphs in 1897 and 1899 there were two other Irish or Irish-connected victories in what was then the blue riband of steeplechasing.

The Widger family of Waterford were well-known — indeed renowned — dealers and breeders of high-class steeplechasers and hunters. There were six sons of the patriarch, Tom Widger, all of whom joined him in the business except William, who became a Franciscan friar. Of those sons the best and most dedicated race-riders were the two youngest, Michael and Joe, whose avowed ambition was to train, own and ride a winner of the Grand National. With that in mind they bought in December 1893 a gelding called Wild Man From Borneo from J. J. Maher for a sum in the region of £600. Maher was to become one of the best known of Irish bloodstock breeders, producing many classic winners, but at that time his main interest was in steeplechasers. He had bought Wild Man From Borneo as a foal and parted with him — oddly enough, in view of the preparation he was later to be given — because he did not think he would stand training. Ridden by Joe, he was third in the National of 1894; his rider blamed himself for the defeat, saying that, not knowing just what he had under him, he had not made sufficient use of his mount.

In the following year the brothers decided to make no such mistake and 'to lay themselves out to win the big race in real earnest'. To this end they crossed over to England and put themselves and their horses in the care of J. Galland at Alfriston in Sussex. Their dedication was well rewarded. Ridden once more by Joe, and landing second over the last, Wild Man From Borneo drew away to score comfortably by a length and a half from Cathal, who was also Irish bred. After the race Galland confided to a friend that he had given the winner such a severe preparation that 'it would have broken down anything save the Wild Man himself, or a traction engine'.

Joe Widger.

It was a real Irish family triumph, and the Widgers and their horse received on their return to Waterford a welcome worthy of it. Bands played; the ships in the harbour were dressed all over with flags; bonfires were lit. One, consisting of twenty barrels of tar, which could be seen, it is said, from Carrick-on-Suir, blazed for a week. Whiskey flowed like water. It did no harm to the Widger family business either. Always popular and respected because of the straightforward nature of their dealings, henceforward they prospered enormously, their average sales in the succeeding years reaching 3,000 horses. Not only did they supply the British army with remounts, but the Dutch and Italian armies were also their customers. In one year alone they supplied two hundred horses to

100

the King of Italy for his personal use. Indeed such was their fame in Italy that they became known simply by the appellation 'I Widgeri'.

A handsome golden chestnut with three white socks, Wild Man From Borneo fell in the Grand National in the following year and was subsequently sold to Miss F. E. Norris of Liverpool, who later became Joe Widger's wife. Increasing weight took its toll on Joe, and after his Grand National victory most of his riding was done in the hunting field. But twenty-seven years later he might well have had another Grand National winner, for his The Drifter was upsides with the eventual winner, Music Hall, at the last when he made a bad mistake and could only finish second.

2

Drogheda, the 1898 winner, described as 'an unpleasant mealy bay', was bred by Mr G. F. Gradwell who lived near that town. He was by Cherry Ripe out of Eglantine, who had won the Irish Grand National in 1887 in Mr Gradwell's colours. Drogheda won the Galway Plate in 1897 for Mr Gradwell, who, it may be mentioned in passing, became a racing official and was Clerk of the Course at Galway until 1929. Later that year R. C. Dawson, who, having failed to buy Eyrefield Lodge, was then about to move his training quarters from the Curragh to Berkshire, met Mr Gradwell after the Dublin Horse Show and bought Drogheda from him for himself and Mr G. C. M. Adam for £1,500 with a £300 contingency if the horse won the Grand National. Dawson took him to England with him and trained him there. The race was run in a snowstorm and the ground was every bit as heavy as in Seaman's year. Ridden by J. Gourley, Drogheda won by three lengths from Cathal, who was thus runner-up for the second time. Drogheda was subsequently sold to Mr Bulteel, for whom he did little.

Dawson, a graduate of Dublin University, had placed himself as a learner in the hands of Linde. He then went into partnership with J. J. Maher, owning and training steeplechasers which were ridden for them by H. S. 'Atty' Persse, a member of the well-known Galway whiskey-distilling family. All three were later to gain the utmost distinction on the Turf. Maher has already been mentioned as the vendor of Wild Man From Borneo. In the years to come he produced two more Grand National winners in Covercoat and Ballymacad and, on the flat, amongst others, Manna, who won the Two Thousand Guineas and the Derby in 1925. Persse, who moved from Ireland to England in 1906, bought and trained that great flyer The Tetrarch and became the most famous producer of two-year-olds ready to run and win on their first outings in his or possibly any other generation. He also trained four classic winners and brought off

R. C. Dawson.

H. S. 'Atty' Persse.

many big gambles in handicaps. Soon after Drogheda's win Dawson turned his attention to the flat and, amongst a legion of winners of great races, sent out Trigo and Blenheim to win the Derby in 1929 and 1930; in addition, Finfinella won a wartime substitute for him in 1916. He thus became the first and only trainer to produce the winners of both the Grand National and the Derby until M. V. O'Brien came along to shatter all records.

3

Meanwhile, in less exalted quarters than Aintree and Epsom, much of the old-style fun and roguery still persisted in Irish steeplechasing. However, the sport was slowly but surely undergoing a process of change and innovation — much to the disgust of diehards like Harry Sargent. These conservatives who looked back fondly to the 'golden age' continued to lament the proliferation of enclosed courses with made-up fences, which they dubbed 'artificial', and the abandonment of the old-time steeplechases over natural courses. To show the difference between the old outlook and what was then the new it is worth while to quote Sargent at some length:

> Oh! were our old rulers and mentors of chase and chasing to look up and see what is now going on, methinks they would go back and contentedly remain where they are! . . . Most of the multitudes who now attend races don't care a jot for the sport; they come only to bet and for the outing. . . . The farmers, as a rule, have not yet succumbed to the infatuation of betting, and still like to see a good steeplechase over a natural country; but they would not give a pin to see one over the cock-pit courses of modern days with their abominable abortions of fences. Therefore they stay away, even if living within a few miles of these artificial hippodromes. . . . I am well aware it was the late Mr Thomas G. Waters who laid out these new courses and remodelled the old. . . . When the old pillars of our sport died or ceased racing, orders went forth to Mr Waters for the pick and spade, the bill-hook and scalping shears to hack and to hew the natural fences, which were sacred from harm in the old men's days. Then came into fashion the artificial courses, which are the great and leading light to the destruction of steeplechasing. . . . All that is needed is to *bring back steeplechasing its original system.*

The Mr Thomas Waters who figured in this philippic was, of course, the 'professional racing engineer' referred to previously as the designer of Cork Park, Tramore and Punchestown. It was he who as far back as 1869, to the fury, we may be sure, of Harry Sargent and his friends, constructed at Ballybrit a complete new

hunters' course with a 'rattling double bank similar to the Punchestown bank'. He also set up fly fences in substitution for the traditional stone walls and laid out a new flat course. In the same year he designed improvements to the stands and the general amenities. In this respect at least Sargent could find it in himself to commend him. 'Although Waters cut the fences down,' he wrote, 'it was he who built up the stand-houses and introduced all the improvements we now enjoy; for which ladies, jockeys, owners, pressmen and all others connected with racing owe him a debt of gratitude.'

A panoramic view of Punchestown in the 1880s.

But for all Sargent's laments about conformity of courses and the lack of sporting spirit, the outlandish still occurred and the fun was still there. Colonel Yardley remembered coming over to ride at a Kilkenny meeting about this time:

> During one of the races the open ditch, built up with dry gorse, was fired either by accident or design, and the horses approached it in a sheet of flame. Two of the riders boldly jumped into the middle of the flame, getting through with falls and considerably scorched, and one of them pluckily remounting won the race. I have further cause to remember the meeting, as my racing breeches etc. were purloined.

And Major F. Herbert, another soldier rider, recounted how he got hold of a grey mare with which I won many races. I claimed her out of a selling race at Cork, much to the disgust of the owner, as the general habit was for the Irish owners to enter in selling races but allow no one to claim their animal. Had anyone the courage to do so it invariably ended in a free fight, in the midst of which the animal was whisked away, and possession afterwards could not be obtained. In this case, luckily, while the fight was proceeding, I had taken the precaution to depute some stalwart friends of mine to secure the mare, and thus scored.

Few races, he says, 'were run without objections, with a free fight as the natural result'. He also tells how at some country meetings the 'starters and clerk of the course generally joined in the sport and accompanied the competitors'. Major Herbert owned and rode a horse called Mephistopheles, christened by the Irish bookies 'My Fist of Fleas'. He was, he says, the worst-tempered horse he ever rode, but a good one when he would try. He was backed to win the Punchestown Grand Military and 'had the race in hand' on the run-in when the rider of the second, knowing the peculiarities of Herbert's mount, waved his whip in his direction and generally created such a disturbance that 'My Fist of Fleas', 'stopping as if shot, set to kicking, and so lost me the race'.

But modern times were coming, and with the new century they finally arrived.

II

Victories Over the Water

1

Both over fences and on the flat the twentieth century opened auspiciously for Irish racing. Unquestionably the greatest event was the victory of the Irish-bred and Irish-trained Ambush II for the Prince of Wales in the Grand National of 1900. Ambush II was by Ben Battle out of Miss Plant by Umpire. He was bred by Mr William Ashe of Narraghmore and was bought for the Prince by Mr G. W. 'Tommy' Lushington.

Lushington, who was named by no less an authority than George Lambton as the 'crack amateur of the day', was equally good on the flat or across country. He was also a clever manager and trainer of racehorses and a good judge of bloodstock. Although born in Kent, he had Irish associations, for his father, a London stipendiary magistrate, had a residence in Ireland and owned, rode and trained racehorses there. Educated at Cheltenham and commissioned into the old 2nd Queen's Regiment, Lushington rode his first races in Ireland, where the regiment was quartered. Soon he decided to send in his papers and to concentrate on training and riding races. He used Eyrefield Lodge as his training base until Captain Eustace Loder himself retired from the 12th Lancers to take up residence there and exercise personal supervision over the stud. After Lushington had ridden a winner at Stockbridge for the Prince of Wales, Lord Marcus Beresford, the Prince's close friend and racing manager, brought him along for a formal introduction and a chat with His Royal Highness. The Prince took one of his immediate fancies to him and asked him to look out for likely steeplechasers on his behalf. Lushington's choices were successful, and soon he was appointed to train and manage the steeplechasers belonging to the royal owner.

Ambush II cost Lushington only 500 guineas, for Mr Ashe did not think much of him. He was not alone in his low opinion of the horse. Sent for sale as a two-year-old, he had failed to make the

Tommy Lushington in the royal colours.

Eustace Loder.

meagre reserve of 50 guineas placed on him. Mr Ashe then offered him to a friend for 40 guineas as a likely hunter, but the friend would not have him. But Lushington's sharp eye saw promise in him, and he bought him. A big brown horse, by the time of the race he had grown to be a strong, strapping steeplechaser, a real 'Aintree type', up to weight and able to carry it.

Eyrefield Lodge at that period was run by a notable team. Lushington controlled the racehorses; Noble Johnson managed the stud, whose interests were soon to supersede the racing concerns; Joe Hunter, the head lad, held the steeplechasing licence; and, some said the most important of all, there was Dan McNally, 'Eyrefield Dan', Linde's former stableman, adviser and *fidus Achates*. McNally had refused to leave his beloved Eyrefield on Linde's death and had remained on to give the benefit in his gruff way of all the lore and experience he had gained from his former master. He was also the holder, though in name only, of the flat-racing licence.

There was in the Grand National of 1900 another fancied runner from Eyrefield Lodge, Eustace Loder's own gelding Covert Hack, who had won the Conyngham Cup the year before in the hands of Loder's close friend Major Hughes-Onslow, one of the best amateurs of his day. Covert Hack was to win the Cup again on his return after the Grand National and, in all, twice more before he retired — a record for the race unbeaten to this day. At Aintree, however, he made no show at all, falling at the first fence.

Tommy Lushington was unable to take the ride on Ambush II himself because he had broken one of his hands so badly in a fall at Sandown some years before that he had been warned that another injury to it might result in his being crippled for life. He was, however, still riding with notable success on the flat. The mount on Ambush II was given to Algy Anthony, another Englishman domiciled in Ireland. Anthony hailed, as many great jockeys and horsemen have done, from the very heart of English steeplechasing — Cheltenham. He had been apprenticed to Sam Darling at Beckhampton, and it was Tommy Lushington who had brought him to Ireland to ride for Eyrefield Lodge. He was immediately successful under both Rules. In 1899, the year before he was offered the ride on Ambush II, he had ridden the winner of the Irish Derby and had already headed the list of winning jockeys in Ireland.

The race itself was an epic one. Another Irish-owned, trained, and ridden horse, Colonel Gallwey's Hidden Mystery, started a warm favourite at 75 to 20 against, but Manifesto, even under the crippling burden of 12st 13lb, was, at 6 to 1, strongly fancied to win again. Ambush II divided these two in the betting at 4 to 1. The riderless Covert Hack brought Hidden Mystery down at the first fence on the second circuit. Coming to the last, Manifesto could be seen to be closing on Ambush II, who was in the lead. But, as with so many

Ambush II, winner of the Grand National in 1900, ridden by A. Anthony.

good horses both before and after him, the weight proved too much for Manifesto to give away on the long run-in. His rider, George Williamson, accepting defeat and realising that the old warrior could do no more, eased him into third place. He had been trying to give the winner 24lb. There were tears in the eyes of many as they watched his brave attempt to do so and saw him go down a gallant loser. But nothing could dim the enthusiasm which greeted the popular Prince's victory; indeed it was greater even than that which was accorded to him when he won the Derby with Persimmon four years before.

The press of the crowd about the Prince as he came down to lead the horse in was so tumultuous that he had to be provided with a close escort of police to clear the way. Seeing him so surrounded, a wag in the crowd called out: 'Never mind, Teddy, I'll come and bail you out!'

The Irish association with this memorable event was, in a way,

110

like Galtee More's Derby victory in reverse, for, to alter Moorhouse's words, save that he was Irish bred and trained, every other association with him was English. But Ambush II undoubtedly owed his strength and development to good Irish grass, and the feeding skills and horsemastership of Dan McNally played their part also in this first royal victory at Aintree.

It was indeed a memorable year for Tommy Lushington, for three months later almost to the day he won the Irish Derby with Gallinaria, trained and ridden by himself. Gallinaria was yet another big winner to be sired by Gallinule, whose successes as a stallion were growing year by year. Lushington's Derby win was achieved at the age of forty, when many are thinking of quitting the saddle even on the flat, and by winning he became only the second amateur to do so. To this day he and Tommy Beasley are the only amateurs to appear on the list of winning riders. Algy Anthony too had occasion to remember 1900, for in addition to winning the Grand National he won the Irish Oaks for Captain Loder on May Race.

The year 1900 was also notable for the fact that a big good-looking colt, a half-brother by St Florian to Galtee More, began to grow to maturity on the Bruree paddocks. Mr Gubbins, who by this time was becoming increasingly incapacitated by gout, called him Ard Patrick, and in due course sent him across the water to be trained by Sam Darling. Darling took care not to hustle the big two-year-old and did not produce him until the autumn, when he won at Kempton first time out. He was lightly raced the first season: he contested only three races, winning two of them and being beaten in the Dewhurst Plate by Major (as he had then become) Eustace Loder's Game Chick. After this race he was put by with next year's classics in mind. His great rival, Bob Sievier's wonderful mare Sceptre, also won twice that year as a two-year-old, her only defeat, oddly enough, being inflicted by Game Chick.

2

At about this time there was an increasing demand for more 'park' courses near Dublin to cope with the ever-growing number of city-dwellers who patronised racing as a gambling and spectator sport. In 1902 Phoenix Park was opened to cater for this demand. The course was constructed on ground at Ashtown formerly used for 'flapping' meetings. Just as Leopardstown had been modelled on Sandown, Phoenix Park was a frank imitation of Hurst Park. Mr J. H. H. Peard, formerly in control at Cork Park, was put in as manager.

A qualified veterinary surgeon, Mr Peard was one of the most knowledgeable racing men in Ireland. He was a friend and associate of Mr W. P. Purefoy, owner of a successful stud at Greenhills, Co. Tipperary, who was one of the brains behind the owning, training and gambling syndicate known as the Druid's Lodge Confederacy or the Hermits of Salisbury Plain. Locked away in a remote corner of Wiltshire, this syndicate, before it eventually broke up, plotted in immense secrecy and brought off some of the greatest gambling coups in Turf history, starting with Hackler's Pride's win in the Cambridgeshire of 1902.

Under the management of Mr Peard, Phoenix Park prospered. Soon it inaugurated the Phoenix Plate of 1,500 sovereigns, then the most important two-year-old event in Ireland. Drawing its attendance chiefly from Dublin city — and its fashionable element at that — it was the sort of course the old sportsmen such as Sargent so despised and deprecated. Indeed F. F. MacCabe, having returned from the Boer War, in which he had served with distinction as medical officer to the South Irish Horse, was moved to write: 'It is the only course except the Curragh where no steeplechases are promoted. Their absence from programmes undoubtedly causes many people to stay away.' Despite these strictures — and a singularly difficult finish to interpret from the stands — the Park, as it came to be known, fulfilled a need and played its part in bringing Irish racing into line with the emerging century. It was honoured in the years 1903 and 1904 by the attendance of the new King and Queen on the occasion of their state visit to Ireland.

3

The year 1902 was also marked by a setback to the start of what was to be one of the greatest careers in Irish racing — that of J. J. Parkinson. Qualified as a veterinary surgeon and learning the art of race-riding from Michael Dennehy of French House, the Curragh, Parkinson had ridden his first winner at Roscommon in 1891. Having established himself at Brownstown House, he had built up a reputation in his profession and had also achieved some measure of success in the saddle, though it was said of him that he was never a natural horseman but earned his proficiency by application and hard work. A disciple of Tod Sloan, he adopted the short leathers and crouching seat of the American jockey and required those who rode for him to do the same. But in 1902 at Leopardstown (Leopardstown again!), as one chronicler delicately put it, 'an unfortunate contretemps when Fame and Fortune was disqualified for bumping and boring brought about a temporary retirement from the Turf'.

Much of this 'temporary retirement' was spent in America, where he became more than ever convinced of the efficacy of American methods of training and riding. On his return and reinstatement

J. J. Parkinson.

after a year's absence he purchased Maddenstown Lodge, which he
enlarged and where he built extensive stabling on the most modern
lines. He also took over some of the French House stabling from his
old mentor Michael Dennehy. Once established in his new quarters,
he began to breed and race on an ever-increasing scale. Winners,
both jumpers and on the flat, poured out from Maddenstown Lodge.
In 1904 he sent out Joe Widger's The Gunner to be third in the
Grand National and, in the opinion of some, an unlucky loser. By
that year, the first after his return, all his 150 boxes at Maddenstown
were full. That year too saw Michael Dawson, now established at
Rathbride Manor, the Curragh, scoring his second success in the
Irish Derby with Royal Arch. For the next quarter of a century
these two great trainers were to send out countless winners and
to straddle Irish racing like the colossi they were.

No. 128/BA8099148   *London 15th Aug 1903*

Lloyds Bank Limited

16, St JAMES'S STREET, S.W.

Pay John Gubbins &   *or Bearer*

Twenty Thousand Pounds —

THE INTERNATIONAL HORSE AGENCY
AND EXCHANGE LIMITED,

£20,000 —

W. Allison

In the meantime there had been another Irish-bred and Irish-owned winner of the Epsom Derby, for Ard Patrick had lived up to his early promise. After running indifferently in the Two Thousand Guineas when, as his trainer says, he had not really come to hand, and then being disqualified for bumping in the Newmarket Stakes – an unusual preliminary for a Derby winner – he scored easily at Epsom, having the hot favourite and popular idol, Bob Sievier's Sceptre, down the field behind him.

By then Mr Gubbins was so crippled with gout that he could not lead in his second Derby winner. He was, however, able to witness an even greater triumph the following year. Like his half-brother Galtee More, Ard Patrick suffered from a suspect leg and did not contest the St Leger. He was sound again as a four-year-old and met Sceptre once more in the Eclipse Stakes, giving her the sex allowance. He beat her again, this time by a neck after an epic struggle. Sam Darling rated him just the better of Mr Gubbins's two Derby winners. He was subsequently sold for the same price as Galtee More, £20,000, to Count Lehndorff, who stood him at his Graditz Stud in Germany.

4

In the early years of the century Colonel Hall-Walker, now an MP for the Widnes division of North Lancashire, had not been idle at Tully. He was said to arrange the matings of his mares from his astrological studies, which occasioned a good deal of amused derision. But if he did so rely on celestial guidance, what the stars told him proved to be remarkably accurate. The figures of winning progeny produced by Tully increased substantially year by year, as the following table shows:

114

	£
1901	770
1902	1,350
1903	4,175
1904	12,650
1905	27,400

The stakes won in 1905 placed him at the top of the winning owners' list in England and Ireland. His English winnings alone amounted to £23,687, a sum which was still sufficient to place him at the top of the list. This feat was accomplished with horses all bred by himself at Tully, and, astonishingly, he had only six horses in training in England. With them he won five races at Royal Ascot, then a record. His home-bred Cherry Lass, by Isinglass out of Black Cherry by Bendigo out of Black Duchess, won the One Thousand Guineas and the Oaks and, in all, six out of her eight races, contributing £13,000 to the winning total. She might well, too, have added to her laurels by winning the St Leger, in which she finished third, had she not been amiss.

Colonel Hall-Walker had in that same year another, though indirect, claim to distinction in the history of the Turf. In 1904 the Aga Khan, then aged twenty-seven, stayed with him at Tully. During his visit he inspected the stud, displaying great interest in its owner's methods of selecting matings for his mares. Some years earlier the Aga Khan had had horses running in his name in India, and now Hall-Walker entreated him to come into racing in Ireland and England and start a stud on the lush pastures of Kildare which had proved so valuable to his own enterprises. The Aga Khan was impressed and encouraged, but business and family matters and then the intervention of the First World War prevented his putting into practice the tentative plans he formed for entering the sport. He continued, however, to study blood-lines, and his friendship with Hall-Walker remained intact. During their meetings Hall-Walker constantly impressed upon him the advisability of diverting some of his huge fortune into bloodstock. It was not until seventeen years after that visit to Tully that the Aga Khan launched out into the purchase of yearlings and the acquisition of the studs in Ireland that were to form the foundation of his many victories and triumphs on the Turf. It is nevertheless to Hall-Walker that the credit must go of awakening and kindling the Aga Khan's interest in the breeding of racehorses which was to lead to the creation of one of racing's greatest and most successful empires. This the Aga Khan himself graciously acknowledged in a letter to Sidney Galtrey, one of the most respected racing journalists of the day, written after Lord Wavertree's death in 1933:

It was entirely due to Lord Wavertree, and my personal friendship for him, that I started to race on the English Turf. I would probably never have been known as an owner west of Suez had he not, during and after my visit to Tully in 1904, urged me to take up racing in England. He undoubtedly gave me much good advice, and up to the last I never took an important decision without asking his opinion.

5

There were other successes besides those of Colonel Hall-Walker's Tully Stud. Captain Greer's Gallinule headed the English list of winning stallions in 1904, and in 1905 he was runner-up to Isinglass, much of whose success was, as we have seen, due to Colonel Hall-Walker's filly Cherry Lass's two classic victories. As it was, Isinglass only defeated Gallinule by a trifling sum, and had Gallinule's winning progeny in Ireland been taken into account, he would have been handsomely in front and would in fact have headed the list for many years.

Gallinule also sired Major Eustace Loder's peerless filly Pretty Polly out of her owner's mare Admiration. It is said that Captain

Gallinule.

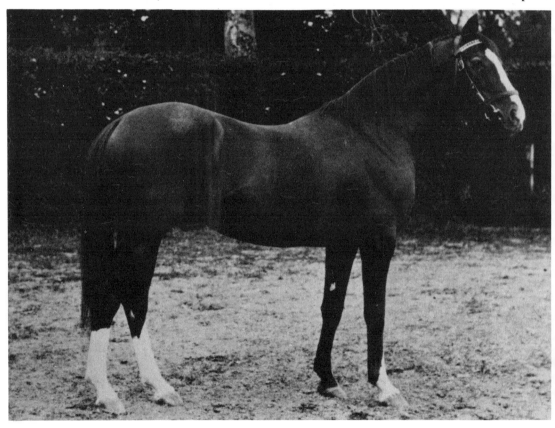

Greer only accepted Admiration's nomination to Gallinule because of his friendship with Mr Noble Johnson, the manager of Eyrefield Stud. Certainly the odds against Admiration producing anything in the nature of the flying phenomenon that Pretty Polly turned out to be were exceedingly long, for she was well-nigh useless as a racehorse herself. Having failed to win as a two-year-old, she won once at three years in a £50 plate at Baldoyle, and during her whole career on the flat she managed to score in only one other race, a £120 plate at Leopardstown. Put to chasing, she showed an equal lack of success, her last race being the Irish Grand Military at Punchestown, in which, ridden by Major Hughes-Onslow, she started favourite but could only finish third to Lord Kenmare's Allumette.

Pretty Polly was sent to be trained by Peter Purcell Gilpin, whose roots, as we have seen, sprang from Kildare and who had by now moved first to Blandford in Dorset and thence to Newmarket following a colossal gamble on Clarehaven in the Cesarewitch of 1900. Pretty Polly's racing career, in which she won nineteen out of her twenty-one races and made herself the darling of the British public, was conducted entirely in England and France and therefore plays no part in this story. It is, however, worth noting that her only defeat in England, in the Ascot Gold Cup of 1906, was inflicted by Bachelor's Button, who was bred by Mr Joseph Lowry of Bachelor's Hall, Navan. Bachelor's Button was by Winkfield out of Milady, and in his early career he was trained by Michael Dawson at the Curragh. Carrying Mr Lowry's colours as a two-year-old, he won the National Produce Stakes, and on his first outing in the following year took the King's Plate at the Curragh. He was then sent to England and, still handled by Dawson, won three more races. It was in his fourth season that Mr Lowry sold him to Mr Solly Joel for £2,300, and it was for Mr Joel that he defeated Pretty Polly in the Gold Cup.

The year 1904 saw the second state visit of King Edward and Queen Alexandra to Ireland. During it they attended both Punchestown and Leopardstown, and at Punchestown saw Ambush II, now a shadow of his former self, run deplorably in the Prince of Wales's Plate. An innovation on the occasion of this visit was the King's use of a motor-car as his chief means of transport; a similar portent of things to come was the arrival that year for the first time at Ballybrit of two motor-cars carrying visitors to the Galway races.

A more immediate foretaste of the future was the victory of Mr P. J. Dunne's Ascetic's Silver in the Irish Grand National, for two years later Ascetic's Silver was to win at Aintree. By then, however, he had passed out of Irish ownership. Mr Dunne having died, his executors put up all his bloodstock for auction. Ascetic's Silver was said to be wrong of his wind, but the Hon. Aubrey Hastings liked him, decided to take a chance on him, and secured him for 800 guineas on behalf of a patron of his stable, Prince Hatzfeldt, a German nobleman who had married American money and raced extensively in England and France. Trained and ridden by Mr Hastings, who had to waste hard to do the weight of 10st 9lb, he well merited the cheers he received as he came home to win by ten lengths. Mr 'Atty' Persse was third in this National on the Irish-bred Aunt May, who was also sired by Ascetic.

As it happened, the winners of the Grand National in all the early years of the new century save two (1901 and 1904) were bred in Ireland: Ambush II (1900), Shannon Lass (1902), Drumcree (1903), Kirkland (1905), Ascetic's Silver (1906), Eremon (1907). But by the time they won they had all passed out of Irish hands and were owned, trained and ridden by Englishmen. Kirkham, the sire of Kirkland, was actually Australian bred, having been sent to England to run in the Derby of 1890, in which he finished down the field. He was then bought to stand in Ireland by the Rev. E. Clifford, who bred Kirkland from him. Drumcree was another son of Ascetic, the supreme sire of steeplechasers of his generation, but Ascetic himself was English bred, being by Hermit (himself a successful sire of jumpers), and had done his racing in England on the flat and over hurdles before being bought to stand in Ireland.

The year of Eremon's Grand National, 1907, was a landmark in Irish racing history. It was in fact a sort of *annus mirabilis* brought about through the unlikely medium of a returned Irish-American with a far from stainless reputation gained elsewhere than on the Turf — Richard 'Boss' Croker.

12

Orby and After

1

Richard Croker was born at Clonakilty, Co. Cork, in 1841, and at the age of seven, at the height of the Great Famine, emigrated with his parents to America. The family settled in New York City, and it was there that Croker fought his way to the top, being successively barman, blacksmith, and professional pugilist until eventually, by successful manipulation of strong-arm methods (or so it was alleged), he became the boss of Tammany Hall, the organisation which controlled the Democratic Party in New York. The position enabled him to amass considerable wealth, and he soon began his racing career, becoming intimate with some of the gaudier elements of the American Turf – Duke, Drake, Wishard, 'Bet-a-Million' Gates, and the like.

In the early years of the twentieth century the American government set up a commission headed by Theodore Roosevelt to enquire into allegations of corruption by the administrators of Tammany Hall. Croker always vehemently denied that it was the cross-examination he had to endure and the subsequent findings of the commission which led to his abrupt departure from America, but, be that as it may, depart he did, reaching England in 1903. On arrival he bought Antwicks Manor in Berkshire as his private residence and set up a training establishment at Moat House near Wantage. Both of these property deals were negotiated for him by Charles Mills, the betting commissioner, and it was on Mills's recommendation that he installed Charles Morton at Moat House as his private trainer.

The association with Morton did not last long. Croker insisted on importing American horses and refused to heed Morton's advice that they would not prove successful on English racecourses. After they had parted, Croker, having learnt by bitter experience the wisdom of Morton's words and always determined to aim at the top, spent 8,000 guineas at the November sales on three choicely bred English fillies. Having done so, he made arrangements to have the fillies trained for him by the Australian J. E. Brewer at Heath House, Newmarket.

Under Jockey Club Rules permission had to be obtained from the Stewards before any horse was allowed to go into training at Newmarket. When this was applied for in respect of Croker's fillies it was curtly refused. No reason was given, but it was clear to all that Croker's supposed antecedents were behind the exclusion. It was further said that Colonel E. W. Baird, one of the Jockey Club Stewards of the time and a kinsman of the rascally 'Abington' Baird, had inspired it.

Furious at his public humiliation, Croker determined to quit England forever. On leaving America he had had no intention of settling in his native land, to which he had previously paid only one hasty visit, but now he immediately sold off the expensive fillies at a substantial loss and transferred all his interests to Ireland. Once there, he purchased the Glencairn estate near Leopardstown and spent £60,000 on making it into an up-to-date racing establishment. With him to Ireland he brought his American-bred stallions Americus and Dobbins and his brood-mare Rhoda B, also American-bred, which he quartered at J. J. Parkinson's stud at French House while Glencairn was being made ready. Parkinson also had charge of the racehorses, and in the years 1905 and 1906 he put Croker top of the list of winning owners in Ireland.

Croker, however, as successive trainers were to find out, was not an easy master to serve. Abrasive and domineering, accustomed to being surrounded by yes-men and having others bend to his will, he demanded his own way as regards the placing and running of his horses and was not prepared to listen to either argument or advice.

2

Amongst the two-year-olds trained by Parkinson for Croker in 1906 was a big rangy colt by Orme out of Croker's own mare Rhoda B. He was named Orby. Although owned by one Irishman and trained by another, it could scarcely be said that Orby was a genuinely Irish horse; indeed on the subject of his breeding it is worth quoting Edward Moorhouse:

> He was bred at Wantage near Berkshire; his sire, Orme, is an English horse; his dam Rhoda B, was bred in America, and bought there as a yearling by Mr Richard Croker; and finally he was reared and trained at Glencairn, six miles from Dublin. It is a moot point, therefore, whether England, Ireland or America, has the right to claim him, and we will not stop to argue the matter.

Orby ran twice as a two-year-old and was beaten on both occasions. It was his second defeat which led to Croker's parting company with Parkinson. The race in question was the Railway Stakes at the Curragh in September, and Orby was beaten into third place by Electric Rose, also owned by Croker. Electric Rose started without a penny of his owner's money on him, while he had backed Orby so heavily that he started second favourite. Since it was the weight of his money which had made Orby start at 3 to 1 on in his first race, in which he had also been beaten, Croker, as may be imagined, was not best pleased. In November he removed all his horses from Parkinson and installed F. F. MacCabe, who had been doing consistently well with a small string, as his private trainer at Glencairn.

Although Orby won first time out at three years, running away with the Earl of Sefton's Plate over seven furlongs at the Liverpool Spring Meeting, Croker convinced himself that he would not stay a mile and a half and instructed MacCabe to take him out of the Derby. An argument ensued, and it took all MacCabe's powers of persuasion to allow the colt to be left in. Even then the matter was not allowed to rest, and Croker continued to dispute his trainer's judgment as to the advisability of running Orby at Epsom. When he won the Baldoyle Plate convincingly, however, Croker finally made up his mind to let the colt take his chance.

Johnny Reiff, an American jockey domiciled in France, whose demure appearance belied an inherent toughness of mind and body coupled with strength and skill in the saddle, was brought over to ride him. In the paddock, according to Moorhouse, none of the competitors looked better than Orby, though Richard Marsh, King Edward's trainer, crabbed him unmercifully, as did several other critics, and he was allowed to start at 100 to 6. Captain Greer's Slieve Gallion, a product of his own stud, being by Gallinule out of Reclusion, who had won the Two Thousand Guineas, was favourite at the prohibitive odds of 13 to 8 on, and Major Loder's Galvani, another Irish-bred, was also well backed as second favourite at 7 to 1.

In the race Orby, though tiring rapidly at the post, won by two lengths. Slieve Gallion, after wandering all over the course, was third. But, to make Croker's cup of triumph full to overflowing, the second horse, Wool Winder, whom Orby had soundly trounced, was owned by Colonel E. W. Baird, the Jockey Club Steward who, if he did not initiate it, was certainly concerned with Croker's banning from Newmarket Heath.

A bunch of cornflowers, as always, at his buttonhole, Croker led his victor in to a tumultuous Irish welcome. Not everyone, however, was so pleased. 'They are taking it very badly up there,' remarked a Jockey Club member in the unsaddling enclosure as he looked at the long faces in the Jockey Club stand. Nor was Croker received by the King, an omission for which he was later to blame MacCabe.

The finish of the 1907 Epsom Derby: Orby, in the centre, beats Wool Winder and the favourite Slieve Gallion.

Richard 'Boss' Croker leads in Orby after his Derby victory.

F. F. MacCabe, Orby's trainer.

Immediately he was free from the congratulations showered on him by his entourage Croker sent a telegram to his housekeeper: 'Orby's won. Hoist the American and Irish flags over the house immediately.' Not to be outdone, MacCabe wired his old regiment, then in camp: 'Medical officer authorises issue of champagne to all ranks.'

Orby was the first and only Irish-trained horse to win the Derby until Hard Ridden in 1958, fifty-one years later, and his victory inspired an old woman to exclaim to MacCabe: 'Thank God and you, sir, we have lived to see a Catholic horse win the Derby!'

Although he was made a Freeman of the City of Dublin (an honour denied to the poet W. B. Yeats, to the indignation of his literary friends), his victory did not make Croker any easier to deal with. Orby had developed a suspect leg, and MacCabe did not want to risk him on the hard ground at the Curragh in the Irish Derby. But Croker, who had been reluctant to start him at Epsom, now insisted on his running. His presence frightened off most of the opposition, and he cantered in, whereupon Croker instructed MacCabe to prepare him for the St Leger. Still worried about the leg, MacCabe protested vigorously that the colt had done enough. His protests were overruled, and, to make matters worse, Croker insisted that Orby should have a preliminary race in the Atlantic Stakes at Liverpool in July.

Against all his inclinations and advice MacCabe started him; he broke down in running and never ran again.

Relations between owner and trainer were now worsening to such an extent that a final break was inevitable. It came when Croker demanded the culling of Hayden, Orby's lead horse, who MacCabe maintained could still prove a useful servant to the stable. The upshot of the argument over this was that MacCabe resigned. In their short association he had won two Derbys for Croker, together with twenty-nine other races and £15,000 in stakes.

Croker now appointed as his trainer James Allen, who had been assistant to MacCabe. Rhodora, with whom MacCabe had won the Dewhurst the year before, was sent out by Allen to win the One Thousand Guineas in 1908, becoming the first Irish-trained filly to do so. She might well have won the Oaks too, had she not been brought down by another filly falling in front of her. Allen, however, did not last long in his new position and was followed by a succession of other trainers. Croker headed the Irish owners' list again in 1911, but he never modified his domineering manner and strident approach, nor was he ever elected to membership of the Irish Turf Club, despite the fact that its members were then more cosmopolitan and less hidebound than their English counterparts. MacCabe, who had served him so well, had this to say of him:

> He wanted his horses always to win and wanted an explanation when they did not. . . . And the hard fact that other people's horses were better on the day and at the weights was no explanation to him. His horses had won before and should always be capable of doing so.

3

In Orby's year Michael Dawson headed the Irish trainers' list for the second time, winning 61 races and stakes worth £9,221, a record until he himself exceeded it in the following year with a winning total of £11,205. He went on to head the list each year until 1914 when J. J. Parkinson, who had been runner-up during his successive winning years, just defeated him.

The year 1907 was also notable for the fact that Colonel Hall-Walker once more headed the list of winning owners in England with his home-bred horses collecting stakes of £17,910, while Gallinule finished on top of the stallions' table, his progeny winning £23,413 and putting him just ahead of St Frusquin. This total did not, of course, include races won in Ireland. By the end of 1907 horses sired by Gallinule had won a total of just on a quarter of a million pounds in stakes.

John Thompson headed the Irish jockeys' list with 53 winners, this being his fourth successive year as champion. He was to top the list again in 1910, 1911 and 1912, when his career was tragically cut short by a fatal fall when schooling over hurdles. Apprenticed to J. J. Parkinson and retained by him every year until his death, Thompson was regarded as a better jockey in sprints than over a distance, though he won the Cambridgeshire on Berrill for J. C. Sullivan when an apprentice as far back as 1900. As required by Parkinson, he adopted the American seat and style and was the first of the leading Irish jockeys to do so.

A photo-montage showing Jenkinstown's victory in the 1910 Grand National.

On a lighter note, it is perhaps instructive, after recalling these triumphs of the Turf and statistics of success, to glance briefly at the other side of the racing coin. As an illustration of this the experience of Mr Lewis Waller, the actor-manager may be recounted.

During the time of Orby's triumphs Mr Waller brought his play *Monsieur Beaucaire* to the Gaiety Theatre, Dublin, where it played to packed houses. When dining one night at the theatre with a leading Irish trainer he was urged to enter racing himself. It was pointed out to him that amongst other advantages it would bring his name before a wider public and help to advertise his productions. Mellowed by the company and the fare, Waller commissioned the trainer to buy him a racehorse. The transaction was duly completed, and the horse was named Beaucaire after the successful play. Unfortunately, when put on a racecourse he proved useless. Some time later the trainer met the impresario and enquired the whereabouts of Beaucaire. 'I saw him only the other day in a hansom,' was the reply. 'He drove me to Waterloo, and I missed my train.'

13

Mostly Donoghue

1

The year 1907 which saw Orby's triumphs also saw the arrival on the Curragh of a young jockey to ride for Phillip 'Phillie' Behan of Mountjoy Lodge. Although overshadowed by the achievements of Dawson and Parkinson, Behan was an astute and successful trainer, especially of two-year-olds. The name of his new recruit was Stephen Donoghue; completely unknown at the time, it was soon to become a household word, and the cry 'Come on, Steve!' would echo across the racetracks of the British Isles and elsewhere. Donoghue was born in Warrington, Lancashire, of an Irish emigrant father and a mother of Irish descent, though up to the time of his engagement by Behan he had not ridden on a racecourse in the land of his ancestors, most of his previous racing experience having been gained, oddly enough, on the country tracks in France.

Charming and feckless, utterly irresponsible as to his obligations to his owners, Steve Donoghue was yet one of the most likeable characters ever to sit in a racing saddle. In addition, he was arguably the greatest horseman of them all, possessing hands which could control the most fractious of horses with a marvellous lightness and strength of touch and persuade them to give of their best. It was this quality of instinctive horsemanship and sympathy with his mount which had brought him to the notice of Michael Dawson when, in 1906, he had paid a brief visit to Rathbride Manor, where his brother George was working, and it was on Dawson's recommendation that Behan engaged him as a likely lightweight jockey.

In his first season at Mountjoy Lodge Donoghue rode about twenty winners, his chief victory being the Irish Cesarewitch on Mrs Lyons, trained by Michael Dawson. By this time Dawson was becoming more and more impressed by the youngster's abilities, as were others. Donoghue had definitely made his mark, and in the next year he dethroned John Thompson and topped the Irish jockeys' list with 46 winners. Owners and trainers were now clamouring for his services, and amongst those whose attention he attracted was the redoubtable Boss Croker.

Lucien Lyne, a well-known American jockey, was that year retained by the Boss, and it was Lyne who was in the saddle when Rhodora won the One Thousand Guineas for him. But, as always with Croker, trouble soon developed between owner and jockey. At Leopardstown in May Donoghue beat Lyne on a fancied horse of Croker's on whom the Boss had had a big bet. Furious as usual when the money went down and was lost, Croker blamed Lyne for the defeat and expressed his opinion in no uncertain terms. From that point on he continued to harry his jockey with all sorts of accusations, with the result that shortly afterwards Lyne asked to be released from his retainer.

Without a retained jockey Croker turned to Donoghue as the man of the moment, asking him to ride for him whenever he was free, and at the end of the 1908 season he engaged him as his first jockey for the coming year at a retainer of £1,000, no small sum in those days.

Croker and Donoghue served each other well — for a time. Donoghue won the 1908 Irish Oaks on Queen of Peace for his employer and was on Rhodora when, as a four-year-old, in September 1909 she slammed Wild Bouquet, the previous year's winner of the Irish Derby. He also rode a host of other winners for Croker.

After her defeat of Wild Bouquet, Rhodora was strongly fancied for the Cambridgeshire. However, as ill luck would have it, Croker, who was present at a trial gallop, was dissatisfied with the result and, much to Donoghue's disgust, asked for it to be run again. The ground was hard, and Rhodora's joints, like those of her half-brother Orby, were suspect; she pulled up lame and never ran again.

But it cannot be denied that it was mainly Croker's horses which put Donoghue at the top of the Irish jockeys' list in 1909 for the second year in succession, once more in front of John Thompson and this time so far ahead that even an illness and an operation caused by a fall from a doped horse — not one of Croker's — at the Phoenix Park did not cause him to forfeit his position.

Nevertheless, inevitably, relations became strained between the pair. Although Croker had first claim on Donoghue, Phillie Behan, whose daughter Donoghue had married the previous September, had a second retainer. Always suspecting the worst of those who rode for him, Croker put his own interpretation on these facts and decided that Donoghue was not giving of his best when opposed by horses trained by Behan. Matters came to a head at the July Meeting at the Curragh when Donoghue on Queen of Peace was beaten by a good filly of Behan's named Sweet Success. Donoghue knew Sweet Success well, for he had himself won races on her for Behan. He warned Croker that they would be beaten, and they were. But Croker, once more bearing out the truth of MacCabe's judgment of him, refused to accept either the form or the running and bitterly blamed Donoghue for the defeat. Thereafter their association became more and more acrimonious. When at the back-end of 1909 Donoghue had to enter hospital for his operation he had come to realise that the partnership was unlikely to continue much longer. He was therefore not entirely surprised, while still in bed recuperating, to receive the following curt missive:

> Dear Donoghue,
>   Please find cheque enclosed for your retainer this season. I shall not require your services for next year.
>   Yours truly,
>   R. Croker

By then, however, Donoghue had little need of Croker's patronage. During the 1909 season he had made frequent visits to England to ride for many of the leading stables, including Druid's Lodge. Most of his engagements came from Atty Persse, now established at Chattis Hill in Hampshire, who had early spotted his brilliance with two-year-olds. Persse now offered him a retainer to ride as his first jockey for the 1911 season. He accepted and left Ireland, never to return save as a visiting jockey — which indeed he was to do very soon and very successfully.

2

The years 1910 and 1911 brought John Thompson back to the top of the jockeys' list in the absence of Donoghue, and 1911 also saw Leopardstown in the news again. The railway strike that year had its effect on racing by curtailing the transport of horses. It particularly threatened Leopardstown, and there was even a current rumour to the effect that the railway workers were prepared to tear up the rails in order to prevent race trains reaching Foxrock station. When news of this was brought to Quin, who was still in charge at the racecourse, his reaction was immediate. Without another thought and without consulting anyone he gave orders to abandon the entire meeting.

Quin had been growing increasingly autocratic over the years, and it was only through the tact of F. Harold Clarke, who had come in as his assistant in 1903, that a head-on clash with the racing authorities had been avoided on several occasions. Clarke had gained his knowledge of racing and its administration during fourteen years spent with Messrs Pratt, the racecourse managers, in London and as assistant to Hwfa Williams at Sandown Park. He well understood the importance of liaison and consultation with the governing bodies, whereas Quin was inclined either to ignore them or to treat them as if they were his minions. Now Clarke went to him and protested that he should not have acted in this high-handed way without giving notice to anyone, either stewards, owners, trainers or public. After a lengthy argument Quin gave way and allowed the first day's racing to proceed. Crowds, however, were, naturally enough, very thin, and the prospects for the following day seemed little better.

Having pondered the matter overnight, next morning Quin returned to his former decision. He gave orders to the staff to close the gates, allow no one in, and to cancel the meeting. It need hardly be said that, having done so, he took no steps to inform the Stewards of the Turf Club or owners or trainers of his decision. Once more Clarke went to him and pleaded with him to allow the meeting to go ahead or, if he was determined to cancel, to follow the proper procedure.

Quin refused to concede anything, until at length his patience gave way and he said to Clarke: 'All right, I'll toss you for it.' A coin was produced and spun, Quin won, and the order to abandon remained unchanged.

A little later Colonel Hall-Walker, now a Steward of the Turf Club, arrived and found the gates locked against him. The Colonel was choleric by disposition, and his temper was by no means mollified by Quin's bland announcement to him that he had ordered cancellation in 'the interests of the public'. There were also furious protests from owners, trainers, press and public who arrived to find the meeting abandoned without any notice being given.

The upshot of the whole affair was that Quin was summoned to appear before the Stewards of the Turf Club, who imposed a substantial fine and ordered him to make good the expenses of those who had travelled their horses to the meeting. In all, that hasty closing of the gates cost Leopardstown over £500, and it is perhaps significant that in the following year F. Harold Clarke was appointed its managing director.

3

On the steeplechasing side there was little of note to report during those years, though the winners of the Aintree Grand National from 1910 to 1913, Jenkinstown, Glenside, Jerry M and Covercoat, were all Irish bred, and the latter two were trained by the Dublin man Robert Gore, who had, however, left Ireland to train at Findon. Jerry M, named after a well-known Irish dealer, had passed through the Widgers' hands before being bought by Gore for Sir Charles Assheton-Smith, a great supporter of chasing, who also owned Covercoat and who had, before he changed his name and inherited a baronetcy, been the owner of Cloister. In Ireland the principal development in steeplechasing in the pre-war years was the inauguration of the Galway Hurdle in 1913, when it was won by Baron F. de Tuyll's Red Damsel from sixteen starters.

Major Dermot McCalmont.

Another great horse brightened that immediate pre-war period, but only the briefest of mentions may be made of him here, since although he was bred by Mr Edward 'Cub' Kennedy of the Straffan Station Stud in Co. Kildare, he spent his meteoric racing career in England. The horse was, of course, The Tetrarch, the 'spotted wonder', probably the fastest two-year-old ever foaled. In 1912 Atty Persse bought him as a yearling for 13,000 guineas. No one then guessed the bargain he was getting; indeed one prospective purchaser was put off by a friend telling him he was wasting his money bidding for a horse whose only prospect was as a likely hunter! Persse quickly passed him on to his cousin, Captain (later Major) Dermot McCalmont, then a serving soldier in the 7th Hussars.

The McCalmont family already had a strong connection with the Turf. Dermot McCalmont was the son of the Captain McCalmont (subsequently General Sir Hugh McCalmont, KCB, CVO) who had objected to 'Bay' Middleton in the Punchestown Grand Military of 1873, and the younger McCalmont had himself won the Grand Military at Sandown in 1911 on his own horse Vinegar Hill. He had inherited a vast fortune on the early death of his uncle, Colonel Harry McCalmont, trainer of Isinglass, who had himself come unexpectedly into great wealth under the will of a grand-uncle, sole proprietor of McCalmont Brothers, a London merchant company.

Donoghue, as Persse's stable jockey, rode The Tetrarch in his seven two-year-old races. He was never beaten, and his blinding speed dumbfounded all who saw him. Considered a virtual certainty for the 1914 Two Thousand Guineas, he was tipped by many good judges to win the Derby as well. Unfortunately doubts to his fitness developed, and he had to be pin-fired during the autumn. Rumour proliferated, but no news, hard or otherwise, came from the stable either to confirm or dispel it. Eventually it was decided that it was impossible to train him further. He was taken out of the Derby and did not run again. The scratching was left very late — 13 May — and caused considerable criticism and controversy. The Tetrarch was retired to his owner's stud at Mount Juliet, Co. Kilkenny, an extensive property which his father had leased on his behalf from the Earl of Carrick.

Donoghue, who knew more about riding the Derby course than most, in later years always maintained that The Tetrarch could not have kept up his brilliant speed for a mile and a half and thus would never in any case have won a Derby, but this did not alter his opinion of him as an equine wonder.

Donoghue's own career continued to be one of unabated success. Back at the Curragh in 1913 and 1914 he won two successive Irish Derbys on Bachelor's Wedding and Land of Song, both trained by his master Atty Persse.

131

*The Tetrarch, Steve
Donoghue up.*

It may here be appropriate to mention that during all this time the Irish Derby had a scale of weights and penalties; it was not until as late as 1946 that it came into line with Epsom, with all colts carrying 9st and all fillies 8st 10lb. But this was not the case in 1913 and 1914. Of Donoghue's mounts, for instance, Bachelor's Wedding carried 9st 1lb receiving 7lb from one runner and 4lb from another, while Land of Song carried 9st 5lb, making him joint top weight with Righ Mor, trained by Dawson.

Land of Song's Irish Derby marked the end of an era. The clouds were gathering, and six short weeks later they burst into flames that were to engulf a world of settled society and fixed values which vanished forever in the conflagration.

132

14

Through War and Revolution

1

At first the outbreak of war in 1914 made little impact on Irish racing; gradually, however, its rigours began to tell. Fermoy racecourse was acquired for military purposes in 1915 and closed down, Cork Park, too, soon became a casualty, being bought by Henry Ford and built over as a factory for his motor vehicles. The old course on the 'back strand' at Tramore had succumbed to the waves before the war, but racing began on the site of the present course under the aegis of Martin Murphy, the owner of the land, and Red Cross meetings were held there in 1914 and 1915.

One course which did carry on without difficulty or interruption was Laytown Strand, situated some twenty-seven miles north of Dublin. Racing on the sands at Laytown continues to this day and is unique in Europe as being the only strand racing to be conducted under the licence and approval of the governing bodies. The first record of these races to appear in the *Irish Racing Calendar* is in the year 1876. According to local tradition, they were originally organised by the parish priest until the arrival of a new and puritanically minded bishop put an end to his activities. Thereafter racing took place at irregular intervals until the early years of the twentieth century, when it came under the control of one of the oldest and best-known Irish racing families, the Delanys, whose colours, black with a gold cap, were amongst the first ever to be registered with the Turf Club. The original enclosure was Paddy Delany's lawn; it has now been moved to a three-acre field abutting the dunes, into which steps leading to it have been built.

The time of racing is controlled by the tide. Three hours before the first race the Clerk of the Course marks out the track on the sand, using poles with red flags for this purpose. The surface is then harrowed and, when the work has been completed, races over distances varying from two miles to a straight five furlongs can be contested. Down the years there has never been a shortage of

Racing on the sands at Laytown, Co. Meath.

runners at Laytown; the erection of marquees gives the affair a carnival appearance, but the racing is serious enough. Leading trainers have run their horses there, and while it is no proving ground for classic hopes, it has maintained its own standard and provided a sporting day's outing for the locals and visitors, amongst whom in 1950 were the Begum and the Aga Khan.

But in the less carefree days of the First World War it became increasingly difficult to organise race meetings. In 1915, when government pressure caused the cessation of all racing in England except at Newmarket, the Irish Stewards had perforce to consider their own position. After much debate they decided to continue racing as before, issuing a statement to the effect that 'The Stewards and Members recognise that the conditions which influenced the Jockey Club to place the present restrictions on racing in England do not affect this country.'

So, in all, ninety-five meetings were held that year, including four in which the proceeds were directed to the Red Cross. The Irish Derby was won by Ballaghtobin, trained by Jos Hunter at Conyngham Lodge. Hunter also won the Irish Oaks, whose distance was for the first time extended from eight to twelve furlongs, with Sir Thomas Dixon's Lathoma. These two victories helped Hunter to the top of the Irish trainers' list, for once breaking the monopoly established by Dawson and Parkinson.

Dawson and Parkinson, however, continued to dominate the Irish racing scene. Their methods of approach to their art were markedly different. Dawson, with the smaller string, preferred to concentrate on high-class horses aimed at important races, while Parkinson was more the dealer-trainer controlling a huge stable of horses, virtually every one of which was for sale. He had agents and spotters the world over; there was a constant traffic of horses to and from his yard; and he cared not how small the race was so long as his runner earned a winning bracket. All this is not to say that he could not train a high-class horse to its best ability when he had one, as indeed his record was to show.

The Irish Grand National was won by Punch, owned by the North of Ireland linen magnate Mr Frank Barbour and ridden by Mr R. H. Walker, both of whose names were to figure prominently in the later history of the Irish Turf; the Conyngham Cup was taken by Minden Rose, owned and ridden by Mr P. B. Bellew, and the Galway Plate by Hill of Camas, owned by Mr W. Molony and ridden by Mr G. Harty. That year also saw the first running of the Irish St Leger, won by La Poloma.

Of far more importance than these events was the decision late in the year by Colonel Hall-Walker to present his Tully Stud to the nation. This munificent offer included all livestock — his stallions, brood-mares, yearlings, foals, half-bred horses, six hundred head of cattle — as well as all forage and implements, and all the furniture, pictures, plate and effects in the house. In return he asked only that the government purchase the land itself, comprising about a thousand acres, and here again he showed his generosity, for the price was to be fixed by a valuer to be appointed not by him but by the purchasers.

At the time of the offer there were no less than forty-three brood-mares on the stud, most of them bred in the purple. Amongst the classics and great races won by the produce of Tully during the fifteen years that Colonel Hall-Walker had controlled it were: the Derby, the Oaks, the Two Thousand Guineas, the One Thousand Guineas (twice), the St Leger (twice), the Ascot Gold Cup (twice), the Gimcrack Stakes (four times), and the St James's Palace Stakes (five times). A host of other winners in lesser races completed a formidable record; yet the government, preoccupied with the furtherance of the war and dominated by members who had little or no interest in racing or the protection of the thoroughbred, hesitated and procrastinated about accepting the gift. Finally the decision to refuse it was arrived at, and Colonel Hall-Walker instructed Messrs Tattersall to dispose of his stud by public auction.

Attempts, chiefly inspired by Lord Selborne, were, however, continued behind the scenes to persuade the cabinet to change its mind, which, at the very last moment, it did. Lord Selborne was authorised to send the following telegram to Colonel Hall-Walker: 'Gladly accept your generous gift of your horses and livestock, buy

Colonel W. Hall-Walker,
later Lord Wavertree.

your properties at Russley and Tully.' The telegram was received by Colonel Hall-Walker only the evening before the sale was to take place. Magnanimous as ever, and despite the fact that enormous offers for block purchases and separate deals had already been made, he instructed Tattersalls to cancel the sale, and his original scheme was put into effect.

Captain Henry Greer was nominated as the government valuer. His estimate of the livestock came to £74,000, while he valued the farms at £65,625. This latter sum was duly paid to the donor. Captain Greer was then appointed first manager of the National Stud, as it was henceforth to be known. Five years later Colonel Hall-Walker was raised to the peerage as Lord Wavertree.

136

The year 1916 began quietly enough, even though beneath the surface turbulent currents were stirring. The Easter Rising broke out while the Fairyhouse Grand National Meeting was taking place, the big race being won by All Sorts. Cork Park too, far from the centre of the fighting, held its Easter Meeting without disturbance. Racing was, however, disrupted and curtailed for a time. Some meetings were cancelled, but Punchestown went ahead, the Baldoyle Derby was run, and in June the Irish Derby, oddly enough in the circumstances, was won by Furore, who was English owned, trained and ridden. In September a new course serving the south was opened at Limerick Junction. In that year too Goffs conducted a disposal sale for Boss Croker, who was having one of his periodic disillusionments with racing. 'I guess I won't buy any more motor-cars for bookmakers,' he said. There were forty-five lots in the sale, and amongst them was a future Derby winner, Grand Parade, who was knocked down as a foal for 470 guineas.

Despite a multiplicity of difficulties during the remaining war years, racing was kept going, though on a limited scale. That it survived at all was chiefly due to the unremitting efforts of two men, Lord Decies, who owned the winner of the 1915 Irish Derby, and Sir William Nelson.

It was, in a way, a strange alliance, for they came from very different backgrounds. Lord Decies was an aristocrat, a member of the Ascendancy and a Steward of the Turf Club; Nelson had had to make his own way in the world and had done so with success. Born in Ireland, he had emigrated to the Argentine, where he had built up an extensive business and made a fortune in killing, marketing and exporting meat. His early racing was done in South America, where he controlled a considerable string of horses. Returning to England at the beginning of the century, he continued to race on a large scale and was one of the first supporters of Steve Donoghue, who won the Irish Derby for him in 1913 on Bachelor's Wedding. At the outbreak of the war he returned to race in his native country.

Fond of the good things of life and the means of obtaining them, Sir William Nelson was a gambling owner, but the reference to him by the then Robin Goodfellow of the *Daily Mail* as a 'dead-meat merchant', which might have referred to the origins of his fortune or to the frequency of non-triers amongst his runners (and was taken by many to mean the latter), was unfair and bitterly resented. Dogmatic and forceful, he liked to have his own way; he wanted his horses to run, war or no war; and it was his energy and drive, combined with the influence Lord Decies could exercise, which ensured the preservation of racing in Ireland during those difficult years.

Once the war was over, the Stewards were faced with the even more formidable task of preserving the existence of the sport through an unprecedented period of insurrection, atrocity and the 'Black and Tan' war. These difficulties were exacerbated by a shortage of coal for rail transport and by a railway strike. Fairyhouse and Punchestown were both abandoned in 1918 owing to the strike, and in 1920 Punchestown was again lost, this time at the last moment, on the urgent orders of Percy La Touche, the Senior Steward.

In all these adverse circumstances racing could not prosper — but it survived. General Sir Nevil Macready, the commander of the British forces in Ireland during the 'Troubles', took upon himself some of the credit for this survival, writing in his memoirs:

> It is curious to note that all through the worst troubles in Ireland racing went on as if the crack of a revolver had never been heard in the land, but at one time the rebels began to interfere with officers who did not see why they should not have their share of enjoyment. After consulting several of the principal racing men I let it be known that on the next occasion on which any soldier was interfered with, either at or going to, or coming from, a race meeting, I would shut down racing throughout the country. The word went around and no further incidents occurred.

This may or may not have been the reason for racing's continuance, but it is the fact that the racing authorities were left free to administer the sport as best they could without official interference, and somehow or other racegoers found their way to the various meetings. The chronicler of Galway described what was happening all over the country when he said that 'thousands of side-cars, traps, coaches and brakes' carried spectators to Ballybrit when there had been a threat to abandon the meeting owing to an expected lack of attendance. Indeed, despite everything, plans were being made at the very height of the 'Troubles' for the establishment of a new race-course at Navan, although its inaugural meeting did not take place until shortly after the truce of 1921. Among its directors were Major T. C. Collins-Gerrard, the owner of Troytown, Albert Lowry of Bachelor's Lodge, and Arthur McCann, a stockbroker. Its first grandstand was purchased for £50 from a racecourse in Wales which was closing down. On his return from closing the deal the emissary sent by the directors to buy it was censured by them for having paid an excessive price!

At Tramore too, when there was fear that the course would close after Martin Murphy's death in 1920, a new company was formed to ensure its preservation. The first directors of this company were J. J. Parkinson, Francis Joseph Murphy and Thomas James Fleming, who together paid £7,000 to the executors of Martin Murphy to take over control. At Galway in the same year another threat to cancellation was avoided by the successful efforts of two of its directors, Mr Martin McDonogh and Mr C. Kerins, who arranged the necessary transport. On the first day of this meeting Harry Ussher trained the winners of all the races except the Plate, which was won by Clonree, trained and ridden by Frank Morgan, a member of the famous Waterford racing family, who had been champion jockey in 1917.

It was in 1920 too that Troytown had his final winding-up race at Leopardstown before going to Liverpool to win the Grand National. Bred in Ireland by his owner, Major Collins-Gerrard, Troytown was by Zria, who stood at the Leggan Hall Stud in Co. Louth. He was ridden by Jack Anthony, one of the greatest Aintree riders of all time. He was trained in Ireland by Algy Anthony (no relation of the rider) and had already won the Grand Steeple at Auteuil and the Champion Steeplechase at Liverpool in the previous year. A great future was predicted for him, but on being sent to Paris after the Grand National, he broke a leg in the Prix des Drags and had to be destroyed.

The continued liaison between the Turf authorities and the military may have been helped by the fact that a soldier, General Sir Bryan Mahon, a member of the Turf Club and the Irish National Hunt Steeplechase Committee and a former commander of the forces in Ireland, succeeded Percy La Touche as a Steward of the INHSC on the latter's death at the age of seventy-five in 1921. Certainly the governing bodies were not only content to carry on, but determined to make what progress they could. Their tenacity of purpose soon bore fruit, for the first running of the Irish Two Thousand Guineas took place in 1921, and the following year saw the inauguration of the Irish One Thousand Guineas. The latter race was won by La Violette, ridden by a jockey whose name was to dominate the Irish jockeys' list for many years to come – Morny Wing. The successful carrying on of the sport was helped too by the appointment of the knowledgeable and tactful F. Harold Clarke as Keeper of the Match Book in 1921.

The truce of 1921 imposed an uneasy peace on the country and enabled those of the occupying forces and their erstwhile enemies to mingle on the racecourse and elsewhere. Brigadier-General Ormonde Winter, the Deputy Chief of Police in Dublin Castle and a racing man himself, has left in his memoirs a vignette which captures something of the air of unreality which hung over that strange interregnum. He had been anxious to capture Dan Breen, one of the leading guerrilla leaders, but had failed to do so. However, he wrote, 'I once rubbed shoulders with him, after the Truce when we were both making a bet with Dan Leahy, the well-known bookmaker, at the Galway Races. I wonder if he had an automatic in his pocket at the time? I know I had!'

The civil war, which erupted in 1922 after the departure of the British, in fact caused more disruption of racing than all that had gone before. Thirty-nine meetings were abandoned; even Galway had to admit defeat, and no meeting was held that year for the first time since the inauguration of Ballybrit racecourse. But Fairyhouse and Punchestown went ahead. The Irish Grand National and the Conyngham Cup for the first time in their histories were won by the same horse, Halston, owned by Major D. Dixon, the Senior Steward of the INHSC, trained by J. Ruttle, and ridden at Fairyhouse by J. Maloney and at Punchestown by Mr L. L. Firth. The 1922 winner of the Aintree Grand National, Music Hall, was bred in Ireland, as had been the previous year's winner, Shaun Spadah.

15

Progress over Obstacles

1

It cannot be denied that between the wars Irish racing, especially on the flat, fell into a state somewhat resembling stagnation. The better horses, such as they were, mostly went to England to race, and the Irish Derby became almost a monopoly of English raiders, who appeared to be able to come over and pick it up as and when they liked. In the decade 1922-32 every Irish Derby except one was won by an English-trained horse.

A stable-lads' strike at the Curragh in 1924, though it was not of long duration, did not help matters. The impact of a betting and amusement tax crippled attendances, and, worse still, there was a widespread suspicion that the control of the sport was not as strict as it should have been.

The appointment of local stewards was left by the Turf Club entirely in the hands of each racecourse executive. It was a position which was sought after for reasons of prestige and was often granted as a gesture to the standing of a local magnate or in gratitude for services rendered rather than in recognition of integrity or knowledge of racing. There were as yet no stewards' secretaries and no stipendiary stewards. In addition to all this, the state of the country remained disturbed and the political outlook uncertain.

Nevertheless there were highlights, and progress was made. The Tully Stud, by then renamed the National Stud, maintained its tradition of producing high-class winners. At the Newmarket December Sales of 1920 it sent up a brown yearling colt by Swynford out of Blanche by White Eagle. The colt was knocked down to R. C. Dawson for 730 guineas, the underbidder being F. F. MacCabe, now returned from service in the second of his wars as a lieutenant-colonel. Named Blandford and never easy to train, he ran only twice as a two-year-old, winning once and going under by a neck in his second race when giving the winner 10lb. This was the sole defeat of his short career on the racecourse. At three years he won the

Paradise Stakes at Hurst Park, beating Spike Island, the winner of that year's Irish Derby, by a comfortable two lengths. On his next outing he won the Prince of Wales Stakes at Newmarket by the same distance. Tendon trouble then intervened, and Dawson retired him to stand at Cloghran Stud in Co. Dublin which he shared with his brother. Dawson always maintained that he was the best of his year and would have won the Derby had he been entered for it, but he had been sickly as a yearling and the classic entries had closed before the December Sales of 1920.

At Cloghran Blandford was to become the outstanding sire of his generation. Before he died the winners of four Derbys stood to his credit, and in 1934 his stock won £75,707, beating the former record of £61,391 set up by Stockwell in 1866.

The first of his Derby winners was Trigo, owned by Mr W. Barnett, a Belfast grain importer. Mr Barnett kept his mares at Dawson's Cloghran Stud, and amongst them was one named Athasi, who had not been of much account as a racehorse. Mated with Blandford, however, she proved an outstanding brood-mare. Her first foal, Athford, won the Phoenix Plate in 1927 and subsequently the Jubilee Cup and the Doncaster Cup. In 1926 she produced a full brother to Athford whom Mr Barnett named Trigo, which is the Spanish word for 'wheat'. As a two-year-old Trigo was sent to be trained by J. T. Rogers at Crotanstown.

Rogers, an Englishman who had settled at the Curragh during the First World War, took up permanent residence there and became a highly successful trainer, winning, in all, eleven Irish classics before he retired in 1937. In his first season Trigo repeated his brother's triumph in the Phoenix Plate and also took the Anglesey Stakes of 6 furlongs and 63 yards at the Curragh. Two days after his victory in the Anglesey Stakes he was brought out again in the Railway Stakes and was beaten by Soloptic, to whom he was giving 18lb. On his return home he was found to be coughing, a fact which almost certainly explains his defeat. Rogers thought the world of him, and when, as was the practice with Mr Barnett's horses, he was transferred to Dawson's care as a three-year-old he warned the travelling head lad to take particular care of him since he was the best horse ever to come out of Ireland.

Trigo was hardly that, but he won the Derby and the St Leger and followed up the latter victory by winning the Irish St Leger seven days later.

The other Derby winners to be sired by Blandford were Blenheim, Windsor Lad, and Bahram, who won the Triple Crown in 1935 and retired unbeaten. When he died in 1935 Blandford had sired the winners of over three hundred races and in that year was champion sire not only in England but in France as well. Athasi produced for Mr Barnett winners of 52½ races worth over £51,000.

2

New courses came into existence during the decade. Mallow, formed at the instigation and under the control of Lieutenant-Colonel F. F. MacCabe, was opened in 1924 to make good to Cork the loss of Cork Park. Unfortunately its inaugural meeting was marred by scenes reminiscent of the opening of Leopardstown thirty-six years before, the transport and turnstile arrangements proving hopelessly inadequate. Naas came into being, quietly and successfully, in the following month.

In 1923 J. J. Parkinson created a record by training 123 winners in the season. His astonishing career continued unabated. A year earlier William T. Cosgrave, the first President of the Executive Council of the Irish Free State and a racing man himself, had appointed him to the Senate along with the Earl of Mayo, Captain Henry Greer and General Sir Bryan Mahon, all members of the old Ascendancy (it is said that he spent hours agonising over whether there was enough 'Irishness' in their ancestry to justify his choice). In the same year Parkinson became one of the first directors of Goff's Bloodstock Sales when it was formed into a limited company under the chairmanship of Mr Edward Kennedy. In addition, he was, as we have seen, one of the first directors of the new Tramore company, and he was also on the board of Limerick Junction. When the Totalisator Board was formed eight years later this remarkable man became a director of it also.

It was a long time before the Totalisator received general acceptance in Ireland. It had already encountered considerable opposition in England, opposition which, if not actually inspired, was certainly encouraged by the bookmakers, who saw in it a threat to their livelihood. There were, however, those who appreciated its advantages and who pressed for its adoption. Sidney Galtrey, the then Hotspur of the *Daily Telegraph* and one of the most influential racing journalists of the day, was enlisted by Sir William Nelson to assist in a campaign for its acceptance in England. Galtrey had already made a study of Pari-Mutuel betting in France. At Nelson's request he drafted a letter putting the case for the Totalisator and urging its advantages for 'the benefit and enlargement of the Nation's horse-breeding industry'. The letter was signed by Nelson and published in the *Daily Telegraph*. A petition for the adoption of the Totalisator was then circulated and was signed by most of the leading owners, trainers and breeders in the country.

At this stage it occurred to its organisers that it would be a good thing to extend the petition to include those prominent in Irish racing. To this end they asked Mr Edward Kennedy to organise the signing and handed him the petition. Mr Kennedy put it into a brief-case and took it with him to the Curragh as the most likely place to approach intended signatories.

It was not to be expected that the bookmakers, whose intelligence service is, as all the world knows, unrivalled, would stand idly by during these manoeuvres. Perhaps with this in mind and in order to avoid any possibility of the petition being filched, Mr Kennedy decided to sit on the brief-case containing it while racing was taking place. Unfortunately, carried away by the excitement of a close finish, he stood up for a few moments. When he turned to resume his seat the brief-case had gone.

'I have absolutely no evidence', Galtrey wrote afterwards (no doubt with his tongue firmly in his cheek) 'that any enterprising and imaginative member of the [bookmaking] fraternity could have been implicated. I only know that they were not likely to go into mourning over its disappearance.'

Despite this initial setback, the petition was reconstituted as accurately as was possible in the circumstances, and pressure for the adoption of Pari-Mutuel betting went ahead. In 1926 a special committee of the Stewards of the Irish Governing Bodies was set up to examine the whole question. Four years later, at the Fairyhouse Easter Meeting of 1930, the first Pari-Mutuel or Totalisator came into operation in Ireland.

Another innovation was the broadcasting of races. The Irish Derby and the Galway Plate were first described 'over the air' in 1929.

3

During the 1920s steeplechasing in England was in much the same doldrums as flat racing in Ireland. It was said of it then by the grandees of the flat that only the 'needy and greedy' went steeple-chasing, and some of these same grandees even referred to it contemptuously as little better than dog-racing.

In its home and birthplace, Ireland, it never suffered the same denigration, and one good result of its decline in England was that many good Irish steeplechasers stayed at home and raced there. Mr J. E. Tyrrell's Clonsheever was one of these. Trained by Harry Ussher, he won the Galway Plate in successive years 1923 and 1924. On the second of these occasions he was ridden by the Welsh

jockey F. B. Rees, probably the finest rider of steeplechasers in a decade of great jockeys. In 1925, when attempting a third win and burdened with 13st 11lb, Clonsheever struggled gallantly into third place, proving himself one of the immortals of Ballybrit. Three years later East Galway shouldered 12st 7lb to win the Plate and in the following year with 12st 10lb was only just beaten into second place.

Another fine performance in this decade was the winning of the Irish Grand National in 1929 by an amateur rider, Mr F. W. Wise, on his mare Alike. Mr Wise's achievement was all the more extraordinary as he had lost a leg in a flying accident when serving with the Royal Flying Corps in the First World War.

Not all the good horses stayed at home. Sergeant Murphy, who won at Aintree in 1923, was Irish bred, being sired by General Symons. He had had his first race in Ireland before he was sold into English ownership to prove himself, at thirteen years of age, the oldest winner of the race.

In 1924 the Cheltenham executive instituted the Cheltenham Gold Cup as the steeplechasing equivalent of the Ascot Gold Cup. Looked upon for many years as a Grand National trial, it was destined in time to fulfil its founders' intentions and to become a true championship and the blue riband of steeplechasing. Its second running, in 1925, was won by 'the Sligo mare' Ballinode, owned by Mr J. C. Bentley and trained by Frank Morgan on the Curragh.

146

Easter Hero.

Ballinode had already won a race at Nottingham and the Grand Sefton at Aintree before Morgan brought her to Cheltenham. He had intended to ride her himself but was suddenly taken ill, and Ted Leader, then at the outset of a great career, came in for a chance ride. Both horse and rider performed brilliantly, beating the favourite, Alcazar, the mount of F. B. Rees, by five lengths. In the following year Koko, owned by Frank Barbour and trained by Bickley under his owner's supervision at Trimblestown, Co. Meath, was sent over to score a second Irish success in the new race.

Mr Barbour, who had a tremendous flair for sensing promise in a young horse, picking it up at the right price and passing it on at a profit, shortly afterwards moved his training quarters from Ireland to Bishop's Channing in Wiltshire, bringing with him a brilliant tearaway he had recently acquired called Easter Hero. Before the decade was out Easter Hero had won two successive Gold Cups in 1929 and 1930 and had caused the débâcle at the Canal Turn in the Grand National of 1928 which enabled another Irish-bred horse, Tipperary Tim, to win at 100 to 1. Carrying 12st 7lb, Easter Hero finished second in the National of 1929 to yet another Irish-bred, Gregalach, whom he might well have beaten had he not spread a plate half a mile from home. Both Gregalach and Easter Hero were by that great sire of steeplechasers, My Prince. Tipperary Tim, a lucky winner if ever there was one, was by Cipango, a St Frusquin horse.

16

Hard Times and Consolations

1

The 1930s were years of crisis in Irish racing. Already hit by the adverse circumstances described in the last chapter and depressed further by the world slump of the late 1920s, racing under both codes suffered yet another blow when Mr de Valera appropriated the land annuities. This act inspired retaliation from Britain in the form of customs duties on livestock and sparked off the so-called 'economic war' which virtually crippled the burgeoning bloodstock industry. Bloodstock dealing virtually ceased to be a profitable enterprise, and when sales did take place the horses frequently changed hands at giveaway prices. Many of the better horses were quickly shipped off to England during the negotiations before the newly imposed duties had time to take effect.

In consequence of all this, stables were reduced, attendances at race meetings fell further away, and the list of fixtures was curtailed. One particular casualty of the 'economic war' was Navan racecourse. Attendances had been falling off for some time, and the 'war', which hit Co. Meath exceptionally badly, sounded its death-knell. It was closed down in 1934. However, certain of the former members of the board were determined that Navan should not die. A new company was formed with Major T. C. Collins-Gerrard as chairman, and such distinguished racing names as Lord Fingall, Senator Parkinson, Sir James Nelson and Mr Joseph McGrath appeared as directors. The company was incorporated under the name of Proudstown Park (Navan) Racecourse Ltd, and its first meeting was held in 1936.

The deepening of the economic crisis of the 1930s inspired a mood of fatalism amongst those worst affected, well expressed by one writer who quoted a renowned producer of steeplechasers as saying to him: 'If we can't sell the horses, let's get some fun out of them.' Many potentially high-class horses were therefore never seen on the racecourse at all, but were confined to the hunting field and point-to-points.

Golden Miller, G. Wilson up.

The domination of the Grand National and Cheltenham by Irish-bred horses did, however, continue. These were horses which had come to maturity during the early years of the decade and had been exported before Mr de Valera's draconian measures went into operation. The peerless Golden Miller commenced his record run of five successive victories in the Cheltenham Gold Cup in 1932. Bred in Co. Meath, Golden Miller, or 'the Miller' as he became universally known, was by a virtually unknown sire, Goldcourt, out of a mare called Miller's Pride. Goldcourt, who stood at a fee of 5 guineas, had never run; he was by Goldminer, who had also never seen a race-course. Goldminer was, however, by Gallinule, and there was Melbourne blood in his pedigree, a strain which many good judges then insisted was the best of all blood in a jumping line.

150

Golden Miller's dam, Miller's Pride, had never won; her best effort had been to be placed second in a £22 steeplechase at Pilltown. But she had Barcaldine blood in her pedigree and had bred at least one winner, May Crescent, owned by Basil Briscoe, then training at Longstowe. It was in fact through the mare that Briscoe was first attracted to Golden Miller. He bought him for 500 guineas as an unbroken four-year-old and brought him to England, where all his racing was done.

Golden Miller was one of the great steeplechasers — some say the greatest — of all time. Apart from the sequence of five Gold Cups between 1932 and 1936 (there was no race in 1939 or he would almost certainly have won a sixth), he won both the Gold Cup and the Grand National in the same year, 1934, a feat that has never been equalled. Moreover, he carried 12st 2lb when winning that National as a seven-year-old, and this feat *can* never be equalled since the top weight has been reduced to 12st. Nor can it be said that the competition ranged against him by the horses he beat was anything other than top-class. Two of the best of them were Thomond II and Kellsboro' Jack, both Irish-bred. Thomond II gave him his hardest race at level weights in 'the steeplechase of the century', the Gold Cup of 1935, and proved himself able to carry 12st 7lb in handicaps and win — when Golden Miller was not there. In fact he once beat the champion at Kempton when receiving 7lb from him. Kellsboro' Jack, the Grand National winner — and a good one — of 1933, was slammed by the Miller at level weights in the Gold Cup of 1935. It is a measure of his stature that in the National of 1933 the Miller, then only a six-year-old, was set by the handicapper to carry 12st 2lb, giving 7lb to Kellsboro' Jack, who won the race.

Reynoldstown, who won at Aintree in 1935 and 1936, was bred in Ireland by Mr Richard Ball of Balbriggan. Like Gregalach and Easter Hero, he was by My Prince, who, incidentally, also carried Melbourne blood in his pedigree. He was bought by Major Noel Furlong, an Irishman from Cork, and trained by him at his establishment in Leicestershire. In the 1935 race he was ridden by Major Furlong's son Frank, so that Reynoldstown's first Grand National victory was a complete family triumph. In 1936, since Frank Furlong had trouble with his weight, the ride was given to his friend and fellow-cavalryman, Fulke Walwyn, now the famous trainer of steeplechasers at Saxon House, Lambourn.

The Grand National of 1937 was won by Royal Mail, yet another son of My Prince. He was bred in Co. Meath by Charlie Rogers, who sold him to Hubert Hartigan, who in turn passed him on to Mr Hugh Lloyd Thomas, a steeplechasing enthusiast, later to be killed in a fall at Derby, in whose colours he ran. An amateur rider of some distinction himself, Mr Lloyd Thomas was attached to the British Embassy at Paris and could not spare the time to make

151

Over the Big Double at Punchestown.

himself sufficiently fit to do justice to his horse. The ride was there-fore given to Evan Williams, later to become one of the most successful Masters of the Tipperary Foxhounds.

2

At home the accomplishments of Mr George Malcolmson and his mare Pontet must be recorded. Bought for him as a present by his mother for 10 guineas as a yearling and named after a master at his old school, St Columba's College, Rathfarnham, Pontet was ridden to victory by her owner in the Punchestown Cup in 1936. Unable to take the ride in the Irish Grand National of 1937 owing to a fall in a point-to-point, Mr Malcolmson offered it to his friend F. E. McKeever, a member of a famous Co. Meath sporting family. Mr McKeever had only recently turned professional after a singularly successful career as an amateur. In 1933 he had headed the combined list of winning amateur and professional jockeys, becoming only the second rider in Irish racing to do this, the other being W. J. Parkinson, son of J. J. Parkinson, who topped the list in 1916.

152

Pontet duly won, and, fit again, Mr Malcolmson was back in the saddle when she won the Conyngham Cup in the same year, becoming the only mare to complete this double and in fact only the second racehorse to do so. (Halston, already mentioned, was the other.) In both these races Pontet had good horses behind her, for on each occasion the second and third places were filled by Lough Cottage and Workman.

After a successful career as an amateur rider Mr Malcolmson, one of the best liked of all Irish racing personalities, became one of the sport's most able and respected administrators. He served distinguished terms as a Steward of the Turf Club and of the Irish National Hunt Steeplechase Committee, where his knowledge of every facet of racing and his fairness in applying that knowledge was outstanding. His sudden death in 1980 at a comparatively early age was a sad loss to his host of friends and to the Irish Turf.

Over the Downshire Wall at Punchestown.

153

Of the two horses Pontet had behind her in that Conyngham Cup, Workman was third in the Aintree Grand National of 1938 and won it in 1939. He was by Cottage, who succeeded My Prince as the leading sire of steeplechasers in Ireland, and who, moreover, carried Melbourne blood in the dam's side of his pedigree. Cottage had a cosmopolitan history and ancestry. He was by Tracery, who was bred in Kentucky by Mr Belmont but was sent to race in England, where he won the St Leger of 1912 and might well have won the Ascot Gold Cup of 1913 had he not been brought down by a man running on to the course waving a flag and threatening the runners with a revolver. Cottage himself was bred in France by Baron Edouard de Rothschild in 1918. Sent to race in England, he won only once, a small race at Doncaster worth £168. He had a savage temperament, and when put up for sale at the Newmarket Bloodstock Sales of 1924 he was knocked down to the only bidder, Mr Michael Magnier of the Grange Stud, Fermoy Co. Cork, for 25 guineas. 'There goes twenty-five pounds' worth of trouble' was one comment as he left the ring. But Mr Magnier tamed him, and he proved the worth of his new owner's gamble by getting not only Workman but also the Grand National winners Sheila's Cottage and Lovely Cottage, the Cheltenham Gold Cup winners Brendan's Cottage and Cottage Rake, together with a host of winners of other races.

Workman himself came from small beginnings. Bred by Mr P. J. O'Leary of Charleville, Co. Cork, he too was originally sold for 25 guineas, an indication of the depressed state of the bloodstock market at the time. When owned by Mr R. de L. Stedman in 1936 he won the La Touche Memorial Cup, run over 4½ miles of bank country at Punchestown. In the following year he passed into the ownership of Sir Alexander Maguire, an Irish industrialist who had business interests in Liverpool. Trained for him by J. Ruttle, he did most of his racing in Ireland, finishing third twice to Pontet in the most important races of 1937, as has been told. When he was third at Aintree in 1938 he was ridden by J. Brogan, and a bad mistake at the second last may have cost him this race. In his victory year of 1939 Tim Hyde, a masterly and versatile horseman, had the mount. This win at Aintree for the first time in many years was an all-Irish one, for the horse was Irish bred, owned, trained and ridden.

3

Irish flat-race horses could in no way emulate these achievements. Indeed the Irish Derby, the articles of which, it should be emphasised, still included penalties, remained a prey to English raiders — many of them failed classic contenders looking for a consolation prize.

Mention should, however, be made of the home-trained Museum, who won the race in 1935 and was the first winner of the Irish Triple Crown. Museum was owned by Sir Victor Sassoon, trained by J. T. Rogers, and ridden in all these classics by Steve Donoghue.

Rogers annexed all the Irish classics that year, for Mr Richard J. Duggan's filly Smokeless, trained by him, won both the One Thousand Guineas and the Oaks. She also ran third in the Irish Derby. Mr Duggan, a leading bookmaker, was a business associate and close friend of Mr Joe McGrath. He was in failing health that summer and was unable to see his filly's triumph in the Oaks. Realising that he had not long to live, he offered Smokeless to Joe McGrath as a present. Mr McGrath honourably refused to accept this, saying that she should be included in the sale of the remainder of Mr Duggan's bloodstock which he had instructed Messrs Goff to carry out. He added that if this were done he would be a very interested bidder. At the sale she was knocked down to him for 4,000 guineas and became one of the foundation mares of his Brownstown Stud.

The career of Morny Wing should also be touched upon, for he was the outstanding jockey on the flat in the inter-war years and immediately after them. Wing, born and apprenticed in England, came to Ireland in 1917. He remained to spend the rest of his life in the country of his adoption and to reign as undisputed leader of his profession even when he did not top the jockeys' list, which before 1940 he did five times. He won his first Irish Derby in 1921 on Ballyheron, owned by Colonel R. B. Charteris of Adare Manor, a member of the Jockey Club as well as of the Turf Club, and before the war broke out he had won it three more times on Waygood, Rock Star and Rosewell.

Like John Thompson, whose record number of jockeys' championships he was later to beat, he excelled in sprints. 'Never leave Wing out in a sprint,' S. C. Jeffery, the supervisor of the Heath House horses, once remarked to Thomas Healy, one of the leading sporting writers and authorities of the day. It was Healy who, when asked to define the difference between a horseman and a jockey, said: 'A horseman is one who *knows how* to ride a horse; a jockey, one who *rides* a horse.'

Healy put the Hartigan brothers, Hubert and Frank, into both these categories, for he held their abilities as riders and trainers to be in the highest class. It was, as he said, bred in them, for their mother was a daughter of John Hubert Moore, and Garrett and Willie Moore their uncles. Frank trained at Weyhill in Hampshire, but Hubert remained at Melitta Lodge, the Curragh, until 1933, when he moved to Penrith. Returning to Ireland, he was immediately successful, and in 1937, by winning £12,372 for his owners, he beat the record Parkinson had established in 1923.

Frank Hartigan.

Hubert Hartigan employed Joe Canty as his principal jockey, and neither of them was averse to a tilt at the ring. Canty's flamboyant lifestyle was the direct opposite of that of his friend, rival and contemporary, Morny Wing. Whereas Wing was serious, dedicated and all but ascetic in his approach, Canty openly enjoyed late nights, bright lights, fast company, and all that went with them. But there was always a touch of genius about his jockeyship. In 1925 he topped the jockeys' list with 117 winners, his average of winning mounts being 34.51, a record which is still unbroken. It is worth quoting what Healy had to say of him:

156

His mount was always balanced. I am sure it is correct to write that in his heyday he knew no superior, particularly in a long-distance race. None excelled him at 'waiting', and his run at a finish was almost irresistible. Another thing: he could tell more about the merits of a race than any other rider I know. I always sought his opinion when in doubt.

Canty enjoyed a wonderful season in 1939, the last before the outbreak of the Second World War. His many fine victories included two classic wins: the Irish One Thousand Guineas on Serpent Star, and the Irish Derby on Mondragon, both trained by his brother James.

But the whole of that season was overshadowed by the gathering of war-clouds. Both Britain and Ireland abounded with rumour and counter-rumour as to the likelihood of the outbreak of another conflagration. Those who anticipated it were branded with the unlikely and misused name of 'jitterbugs'. The Beaverbrook press and others persisted in maintaining a misplaced euphoria. In September Hitler invaded Poland. Mr Chamberlain announced that a state of war existed between Great Britain and Germany. Ireland declared and maintained its neutrality. The period of the 'phoney war' began.

17

The Second World War

1

At first the war made little difference to the conduct of racing in Ireland, although Red Cross steeplechases were run. The first of these, at Baldoyle, went to Mr Larry Egan's Jack Chaucer, who also won the Irish Grand National. In March 1940 an Irish-bred horse, Bogskar, was the winner of the Aintree Grand National, the last to be run until 1946. In June, when Hitler's Panzers had overrun France and driven the British Expeditionary Force into the sea at Dunkirk, the Irish Derby was won by Turkhan, ridden by the irrepressible Charlie Smirke, who also won the Irish Oaks on the Aga Khan's Queen of Shiraz.

Smirke remained in Ireland for a short time before joining the army, riding for Gerald 'Ginger' Wellesley, who was at that time training for the Aga Khan. After he enlisted he was posted to Northern Ireland and from time to time came south on special leave to ride Wellesley's horses. These expeditions came to an end when he was beaten on a hot favourite, Mah Iran, in a two-year-old race at the Curragh, the whole regiment from the colonel downwards having been on him to a man. When he returned it was explained to Smirke that further applications for racing leave would not be granted and that in refusing them the colonel 'was acting with the best interests of the regiment at heart'.

Mah Iran may have been unlucky to have been beaten, for she was a well-bred filly, being by Bahram out of Mah Mahal. At stud she produced, amongst others, Migoli, who was second in the Derby, third in the St Leger and won the Eclipse Stakes, the Champion Stakes and the Prix de l'Arc de Triomphe. She was also the grand-dam of Petite Etoile.

Later Smirke went with his regiment to Sicily, where his exploits led to the apochryphal story which he told against himself. Frank Butters, an autocratic trainer of the old school, was then in charge of the Aga Khan's horses in England. Butters and Smirke, as perhaps

158

Finish of a race at the Phoenix Park.

was only to be expected, never got on, and Butters, always suspicious of his jockeys, was especially so of Smirke.

One morning during the Sicilian campaign Butters was watching his horses work on the Limekilns at Newmarket. A passing friend called out to him: 'Have you heard that Charlie Smirke has won the VC for stopping a tank?'

'I'm not in the least surprised,' was the reply. 'When he was riding for me he would stop anything.'

But Smirke, when he returned from the war, was also to return to Ireland and, a little later, to write another page into Irish racing history.

2

As time progressed the impact of war began to bite home, and the year 1941, when the news was it its grimmest, looked like being disastrous for Irish racing interests. The supply of foodstuffs was curtailed, rationing was introduced, and there was an outbreak of foot-and-mouth disease. The spread of the disease led to a

159

Going racing during 'the Emergency', showing the variety of horse-drawn transport used.

government order banning all racing from 26 March 1941. Punchestown and Fairyhouse were immediately cancelled. In the event the outbreak was not as serious as had been anticipated and was soon brought under control, but this did not have the effect of producing a rescinding of the ban. Thereupon the Stewards of the two Governing Bodies, accompanied by representatives of other interested parties, waited on the Ministry for Agriculture and put before him their case for a resumption of racing, at least on a limited scale. The minister yielded to their arguments to the extent of indicating that he would grant licences to executives who applied for permission to race, provided he was satisfied as to their bona fides and that a real need was being fulfilled.

Although the Irish Grand National and the Conyngham Cup were irretrievably lost, the Galway Plate was run and won by Miss M. O. Mathieson's St Martin, trained by Cecil Brabazon and ridden by his son Aubrey. All the classics too were successfully run at the Curragh,

160

the Irish Derby going to one of its less distinguished winners, Sol Oriens, owned by Mr A. P. Reynolds, chairman of CIE, the state-owned transport monopoly, who raced under the *nom de course* of J. Dillon, a practice still permitted by the Turf Club. Sol Oriens was ridden by G. Wells and trained by Colonel A. J. Blake, a nephew of Charles Blake, whom he had succeeded in charge of the Heath House establishment at Maryborough.

In 1942 there came a further and graver threat to racing. The country was in the grip of a severe shortage of petrol, which meant an almost complete absence of transport both for horses and for the public who wished to attend and watch them run. Many were the devices resorted to in order to overcome this. The horse came into his own again as a substitute for the internal combustion engine, and carriages, cabs, traps, shooting-brakes were all discovered in the depths of old coach-houses and stables, renovated and pressed into service. Nevertheless the number of meetings had perforce to be reduced, and those that were held became more centralised.

Despite these drawbacks and handicaps, the year was distinguished by the fact that two great horses, one on the flat and the other a steeplechaser, reached their peak and brightened the dark days by their performances. Their names were Windsor Slipper and Prince Regent.

3

Windsor Slipper was owned by Mr Joseph McGrath, who was to become the leader of his generation in Irish racing and well able to rank with those other colossi, Lord Drogheda and C. J. Blake, whose achievements as an owner in fact he far surpassed. McGrath had served as Minister both for Agriculture and for Industry and Commerce in Mr Cosgrave's government. In 1930, in conjunction with Captain Spencer Freeman and Richard Duggan, the successful bookmaker already mentioned as the owner of Smokeless, he had launched the Irish Hospitals Sweepstakes, which proved immensely profitable for its originators as well as benefiting the charitable object to which it owed its conception. Soon afterwards, as a result of Duggan's encouragement, McGrath entered racing. Joe McGrath was a dynamic personality, a masterly administrator endowed with an immense capacity for sustained hard work, and his industry and energy drove him to the top in all he did. By 1941 he had almost reached it in racing, and 1942 put him there.

In 1939 McGrath had bought from Lord Furness a colt by Windsor Lad out of Carpet Slipper. Owing to the imminence of war, this colt, whom he named Windsor Slipper, came to him relatively cheaply and proved a wonderful bargain. Trained by M. C. Collins, as a two-year-old Windsor Slipper was unbeaten. In the same year McGrath purchased the historic Brownstown Stud on the Curragh, from which as his headquarters he was later to develop what was probably the greatest racing and breeding empire Ireland has ever seen.

As a three-year-old Windsor Slipper, without a preliminary race, won the Irish Two Thousand Guineas with supreme ease and then went on to become the second winner of the Irish Triple Crown, never being seriously challenged in either of the two later Irish classics. He could never, of course, be raced outside Ireland owing to the war, and after his final victory he was retired unbeaten to the Brownstown Stud. Because of the war and because he was never extended, it is impossible to say just how good Windsor Slipper was. What is undeniable is that he was very very good indeed. Morny Wing, who rode him, rated him amongst the greatest racehorses of all time, saying, possibly with some hyperbole, that he was the best horse ever to have raced in Ireland.

Shortly before Windsor Slipper began his unbeaten career Morny Wing had been retained by Joe McGrath as his first jockey at a figure said to be the largest ever given to a jockey in Ireland. Whatever the figure was, he certainly justified it. He was champion jockey in 1941 and 1942 and remained at the top of the list for the next three years. Joe McGrath was leading owner for five successive years until 1947, when he was second to Mr J. McLean. Although defeated that year, he nevertheless won twenty races with eleven horses, which was more than any other owner achieved, though the veteran J. J. Parkinson ran him close with nineteen. These bare statistics alone show the extent to which McGrath dominated the Irish flat-racing scene from the days of Windsor Slipper onwards, and further triumphs were still to come.

4

The steeplechaser who brightened the dark days of the first half of that fateful year of 1942, when all seemed to be going wrong for the West and Hitler to be ever more in the ascendant, was Mr J. V. Rank's Prince Regent.

Prince Regent was a great steeplechaser by any standard, and it remains a tragedy that the war prevented him from demonstrating that greatness in cross-channel competition. Nevertheless what he accomplished at home is sufficient to entitle him to enter the ranks reserved for the elect, since the general wartime embargo on the international transport of bloodstock meant that he was opposed in Ireland by competitors of a far higher standard than would have been the case in ordinary times.

Bought as a yearling at the Ballsbridge Sales of 1935 for 320 guineas by the milling millionaire Mr J. V. Rank, Prince Regent was

by My Prince out of Nemaea, a full sister to a good sprinter, Diomedes. Nemaea had cost Mr A. H. Maxwell of the Corduff Stud, Lusk, Co. Dublin, 30 guineas as a foal at Ballsbridge in 1921. She was useless as a racehorse and was soon taken out of training. Before she foaled Prince Regent in April 1935 when she was fourteen she had bred Mr Maxwell at least one other winner by My Prince. Mr Rank boarded him out with Mr Robert Power, MRCVS, until he was three and then sent him to T. W. Dreaper at Greenogue, Kilsallaghan, Co. Dublin, to be trained. He was fortunate in his choice, for Mr Dreaper, then a young man, was a horseman himself who combined an innate understanding of the horses in his care with an absolute refusal to hurry them for financial or any other reason; he was soon to prove

Prince Regent, his trainer, rider and owner. l to r., T. W. Dreaper, Tim Hyde, J. V. Rank.

163

himself one of the outstanding trainers of steeplechasers in modern times.

A big bay horse — he stood 16.3 hands — full of quality, at three years Prince Regent was still unfurnished, and Mr Dreaper determined to give him time. So it was that the first occasion he saw a racecourse was as a five-year-old, when he was twice unplaced on the flat before winning over 1½ miles at Naas with his trainer in the saddle. In the next season, 1941, he won three races, one of them a hurdle, but his trainer still refused to hurry him. In 1942, at seven years, he really came into his own. It was as well for him that he did, for he had to face fierce competition. From the middle of that season onward he was ridden by Tim Hyde in all his steeplechases, and Hyde has placed it on record that owing to the war 'It was the heyday of Irish steeplechasing, with good horses a penny a dozen.' Amongst them two were outstanding. These were Golden Jack, by Goldcourt, Golden Miller's sire, who was owned by the eccentric millionairess Miss Dorothy Paget, and Prince Blackthorn, then a rising and brilliant four-year-old.

Because of the restrictions on racing in England during the war, Miss Paget had sent her steeplechasers to Ireland to be trained. She had no inhibitions about running her horses early, and Golden Jack, although the same age as Prince Regent, had been brought to hand sooner and gained his experience earlier than Prince Regent was asked to do. He had been the champion novice chaser in Ireland in 1941, winning nine races, including the Avonmore Steeplechase over an extended three miles at Leopardstown, in which he had beaten the still inexperienced Prince Regent by a short head when giving him 15lb. Nevertheless Prince Regent won three of his four races that year, the Leopardstown race being his only defeat, and his performances so impressed the handicapper that in 1942 he set him to carry 12st or over on each of his appearances.

Prince Regent defied these impositions by winning handsomely on each of his early outings. He won the Press Handicap Steeplechase over an extended three miles at Naas by twenty lengths carrying 12st 2lb, the Ardmulcham Steeplechase of three miles at Navan by eight lengths carrying 12st 7lb, the Baldoyle Steeplechase of three miles by half a length under 12st 7lb. As a result of these performances, he was asked to carry 12st 7lb in the Irish Grand National and concede 12lb to Golden Jack, an interesting reversal of the previous year's handicapping. He accomplished all that was asked of him and beat Golden Jack by a length. In his last appearance that year, the Avonmore Steeplechase at Leopardstown, the handicapper handed him the crippling burden of 12st 12lb over an extended three miles. The task of giving Prince Blackthorn no less than 3st 5lb and another good horse On The Go 2st 6lb proved just too much for him and he finished third.

Tim Hyde always rated Prince Blackthorn as the best horse Prince

Regent raced against in Ireland. The two met again at Baldoyle in January of the following year, when Prince Regent was asked to give the younger horse 2st 11lb. Then just turned five years, Prince Blackthorn came to this race with a growing reputation, for, in addition to his defeat of Prince Regent at Leopardstown, he had also trounced Golden Jack when they had met in the previous year. He was held to be possessed of blinding speed, and at the difference of the weights many believed that he would take Prince Regent off his feet. Crowds flocked to see the race, and they were not to be disappointed, for a tremendous struggle developed between the two brilliant horses. Prince Blackthorn headed his rival as they approached the last and was shouted home a winner. But at that point Prince Regent showed what a true champion could do. Hyde set him alight. He got to Prince Blackthorn's quarters and was level with him when they jumped the last. Up the straight they battled it out amid a storm of excited cheering from the crowd. Prince Regent came to the other, caught him, and stayed on to win by a neck one of the best steeplechases ever seen in Ireland.

On his next outing, also at Baldoyle, Prince Regent had the speed to win over two miles carrying 12st 9lb and giving 3st 7lb to the runner-up.

It would be tedious to recapitulate in detail Prince Regent's subsequent career. Suffice it to say that, owing to the absence of weight-for-age or conditions races in Ireland at the time, he automatically handicapped himself to carry 12st or over every time he ran and that he carried these weights like the champion he was. Although he was beaten twice in the Irish Grand National, these defeats could in no way tarnish his name or reputation, for in 1943, when beaten by Golden Jack into second place, he was giving him 2st 4lb, and in the following year, when giving another good horse, Knight's Crest, no less than 3st, he only went under by a length. The magnitude of what he accomplished may be measured by the facts that during those years 1943-44 he only once carried less than 12st 7lb over three miles, won five times out of ten starts in steeplechases, and was never giving away less than the 2st 4lb which, as already mentioned, he conceded to Golden Jack in the 1943 Irish Grand National. On the other four occasions the weight difference was 3st. After the war he was sent to race in England, but by that time he was past his best. The twilight of his great career will be dealt with in the next chapter.

5

The prevailing gloom of these years was undoubtedly brightened a little by the achievements of the mighty Prince Regent, whom the public came to see as best they could on bicycles or horse-drawn

Mrs Dermot McCalmont leading in her husband's Piccadilly after his victory in the 1945 Irish Derby.

vehicles or, sometimes, on combustion engines fuelled by coal gas. Meanwhile the war dragged wearily on, besetting racing with numerous difficulties; yet in spite of these, in flat racing as in steeple-chasing, some spectacular successes were being recorded.

In 1943 Joe Canty added further classic victories to his record by winning the Irish Two Thousand Guineas and Derby on Mr F. S. Myerscough's The Phoenix. In 1944 and 1945 came two successive victories for Major Dermot McCalmont in the Irish Derby with the home-bred half-brothers Slide On and Piccadilly.

Hitherto most of Major McCalmont's racing had been done in England, but the advent of war confined his activities to the Irish Turf. A member of the Jockey Club as well as of the Turf Club, he has been noted by the authors of a recent history as being 'more respected than liked among the racing community'. This may well be an accurate assessment, but, be that as it may, no one can deny him the successes which came from the runners produced by the Mount Juliet Stud in Co. Kilkenny, which he conducted on the most lavish lines. Mention has already been made of his phenomenal flyer, The Tetrarch, who had carried his colours just before the First World War. Retired to stud at Mount Juliet, The Tetrarch had got for his owner Tetratema, who won the Two Thousand Guineas at Newmarket and who in turn sired Mr Jinks. Named after an obscure Irish politician whose fortuitous absence from an important vote saved a government, Mr Jinks credited his owner with another classic victory by winning the Two Thousand Guineas for him once more in 1929. In Ireland Major McCalmont had already won the Irish Two Thousand Guineas with Fourth Hand in 1927, and in 1938 he won the Irish One Thousand Guineas with Lapel.

Unquestionably 1944 was Major McCalmont's year in Irish racing, for as well as winning the Derby, he also saw his colours carried to victory in the Irish Oaks by Avoca, a filly by Mr Jinks. It was fitting too that these achievements coincided with Major McCalmont's first year as a Steward of the Turf Club.

During that year the Stewards had many problems to grapple with, the chief being the further curtailment of racing, which led to one Curragh fixture being transferred to the Phoenix Park. Those executives who were permitted to hold meetings found themselves facing a glut of runners, many of them of indifferent quality. To such an extent did this interfere with the control and administration of meetings that application was made to the government to extend the fixture list. This request was granted in a limited form in that permission was given for the holding of certain additional meetings which were designated 'substituted meetings'. The profits derived from these were paid into a central fund. From this fund grants were made from time to time to those executives who had been obliged to cancel their meetings, so that their stands and courses could be maintained in a proper condition for racing to take place when things returned to normal.

It was a far-seeing gesture and showed that the authorities had the future of the sport in mind. But better still was the action taken in respect of the conditions in the classic races. It was decreed that as and from the end of the 1945 flat-racing season no penalties would apply in any of the five Irish classics. The new articles provided that colts would carry 9st and fillies 8st 10lb in the three 'open' classics, from which geldings would in future be excluded. In the fillies' races all the runners would carry 9st. Thus, at a stroke, the Irish classics were immediately raised in importance and prestige, for, as Thomas Healy wrote, 'Whilst a penalty clause was incorporated in the classics, they could be so termed merely as a courtesy, not by right of their status; but when weight terms are strict weight-for-sex the crack three-year-old tests really are classics.'

6

As 1945 drew on and peace became probable many more changes and innovations took place. In 1943 the British government had removed all its stock from Tully to Gillingham in Dorset, where it set up its own National Stud. The land and buildings were handed back to the Irish government, but they remained unused during the war years. It was now decided to establish a new National Stud, and a first Board of Directors was constituted with authority to restock the stud and control its destinies.

Even more important was the passing of the Racing Board and Racecourses Act. This set up a board of eleven members, six of them to be drawn from the Turf Club and INHSC, whose existence as governing bodies was now given official recognition. The board took over the functions of the former Totalisator Board, which was abolished. The act was detailed and comprehensive; its principal provisions related to the powers of the Racing Board, which was given control of the finances of racing and was made responsible for the overall supervision of the racecourse executives, who were in future required to furnish it with annual accounts. Stakes, admission charges, transport of runners, catering, entry fees, prize money, grants for amenities and improvements, all these came within its powers and under its surveillance. This significant reform was indeed a landmark in the history of Irish racing.

The first chairman of the Racing Board was Mr Justice Wylie. W. T. Cosgrave and Joe McGrath were other prominent and authoritative members, and in the following year Mr Cosgrave succeeded Judge Wylie as chairman.

Another important innovation in 1945 was the appointment of T. F. R. Ryan as Stewards' Secretary. His duties were to assist local stewards and advise them in the hearing of enquiries and on the exercise of their disciplinary powers. A racing commission which had been set up in 1942 to look into all aspects of racing, and which in the opinion of many had accomplished little of value, had recommended the appointment of a 'stipendiary' or paid steward to act with local stewards and exercise equal powers, as was done in many foreign countries. The English practice, however, of having a stewards' secretary acting in a purely advisory capacity, which had been established some years before and had been seen to be working well, was preferred as more suitable to the conditions of Irish racing. Mr Ryan commenced his duties at Limerick on 26 December 1945.

For the record, in 1945 Mr Joe McGrath was leading owner once again with seventeen winners of twenty-eight races, his trainer, M. C. Collins, was leading trainer, and his jockey, Morny Wing, leading rider. Major T. C. Collins-Gerrard and Mr Julius Solomon, breeders of Troytown and Golden Miller respectively, died. So also did Steve Donoghue, suddenly, from a heart attack. F. Harold Clarke retired as Keeper of the Match Book after fifty-six years' association with racing. An Irish-bred, Chammoissaire — one of the last products of Tully before it closed down — won the St Leger, run at York instead of Doncaster, and an era came to an end.

18

The Post-War Years

1

The years immediately after the war were notable for the upsurge in attendances both in Ireland and in Great Britain. In 1946 the stake money in Ireland for both branches of the sport totalled a record of £184,562, which by 1950 had increased to £274,554. By 1950, too, a sum of £300,000 had been given by the Racing Board to various executives for improvements to tracks and amenities, and much progress had been made in the installation of camera equipment for the recording of finishes at the principal meetings. In the following year a further £100,000 was spent on improvements, including a new stand at the Curragh, though progress on its construction was hampered by a continuing shortage of materials, especially steel. By that year the photo-finish camera was fully operational at the Curragh, Phoenix Park and Baldoyle, and plans were announced for its installation on other major courses, beginning with Leopardstown and Naas, as soon as the necessary equipment became available.

Much had happened in the meantime. Country meetings thrived. Racing was revived at Roscommon, and in 1948 there was a three-day meeting at Killarney. Continuing disorganisation on the English railways, coupled with danger from floating mines in the Irish Sea, had hindered the easy access of Irish horses to English meetings in the early post-war period. Having received no immediate offers of riding engagements from his former employers, Charlie Smirke had on demobilisation returned to Ireland to ride for Gerald Wellesley. He celebrated his return by riding a couple of hurdle winners and then took the Irish Oaks on Linaria; but when he and Wellesley decided to send Mr Norman Watchorn's crack sprinter The Bug to run in the July Cup at Newmarket, it took three days' travelling to get him there.

Nevertheless in 1946 it was an Irish-bred colt who took the first post-war Derby at Epsom. This was Airborne, bred at Lieutenant-

Colonel Harold Boyd-Rochfort's Middleton Park Stud in Co. Westmeath. A grey colt, Airborne had, a long way back in his pedigree, none other than Tom Ferguson's handsome grey Rust, who had figured prominently in Lottery's Grand National of 1839. This is of interest since when Airborne himself went to stud he proved a failure save as a sire of steeplechasers, getting, amongst others, the grey mare Flying Wild, one of the few horses to defeat the immortal Arkle.

Morny Wing being led in after winning the 1947 Irish St Leger on Esprit de France, owned by Prince Aly Khan and trained by Hubert Hartigan.

At home Joe McGrath and Morny Wing continued their domination of the flat, Wing retiring in 1949 after heading the list for the last time with 51 winners. Joe McGrath's breeding empire, aided by the purchase of Nasrullah for 19,000 guineas, continued to prosper. Nasrullah got Nathoo, winner of the Irish Derby of 1948 for the Aga Khan, in which race, incidentally, Charlie Smirke, who rode the Gaekwar of Baroda's Star of Gujrath into second place, was fined 50 guineas on a report from the starter, Major J. H. Tyrrell,

171

that he had attempted to anticipate the start. Nasrullah's stud career was remarkably successful; he was eventually exported to the United States, but he made an indelible mark on this side of the Atlantic. He was champion sire in 1951 and got the classic winners Musidora, Belle of All, Nearulla and Never Say Die and, of course, winners of countless other races.

2

On the steeplechasing scene the immediate post-war years were dominated by Irish horses. In 1946 Prince Regent, now eleven, was aimed at the big English prizes, the Cheltenham Gold Cup and the Grand National. It had always been the supreme ambition of Mr J. V. Rank's life to win the Grand National, and it looked very much that year as if Prince Regent could achieve it for him. He took the Gold Cup, at that time still regarded as a stepping-stone to the National, with what appeared to be contemptuous ease, brushing aside the only challenge to him which came from another Irish-bred, Poor Flame. After this he was confidently expected to add the Grand National to his laurels, even under the 12st 5lb which the handicapper allotted him.

. But for one person, the man who knew him best, his rider Tim Hyde, doubts were already there. 'In my heart', he wrote afterwards, 'I felt that at last the edge was beginning to go off the great horse's speed . . . and I realised that now, at eleven, he was past his best.' When he dismounted in the unsaddling enclosure at Cheltenham after winning the Gold Cup he hinted as much to his trainer. 'It took me a minute or two to beat that fellow today, Tom,' he said.

Still, public confidence behind Prince Regent remained so great that he started favourite at Aintree at the short price of 9 to 4 against. To Hyde's astonishment he found in the race that his mount was having difficulty in adapting himself to the Aintree fences. During the second circuit Hyde could scarcely believe he was still on his feet, so many were the mistakes he had made. To make matters even worse for him, he was hampered by the constant attentions of loose horses, so that Hyde said afterwards that he had had to ride three finishes to keep in the race at all. Despite everything, he jumped the last in front, but all these adverse factors combined to defeat even his great heart and strength. Lovely Cottage, receiving 25lb, caught up with him and ran him out of it on the flat. When he saw defeat was inevitable Hyde eased him. Another horse, Jack Finlay, also passed him, and Prince Regent finished third.

Lovely Cottage, as his name implies, was by Cottage. The story is told that an English trainer came to Fermoy, Co. Cork, to buy him and, fearful of Irish hospitality, on being offered whiskey, contented

himself with drinking milk instead. He went away having refused to divide the last £100 and afterwards declared that had he drunk the whiskey he would have had the courage to do so and that it all proved that no one could buy horses in Ireland — on milk!

A tired Prince Regent, gallant in defeat, jumping the last fence in the 1946 Grand National.

Prince Regent returned to Liverpool later in the year for the Champion Steeplechase, a weight-for-age race. His reputation was such that he frightened away all opposition except Golden View II, who had won the Irish Grand National in his absence that year, and MacMoffat, who had been second in the Nationals of 1939 and 1940. Both of his opponents fell, and he cantered home alone and at his ease.

Despite difficulties of travel at that Liverpool meeting, Irish horses not only won the Champion Steeplechase but also filled all three places in the Molyneux Steeplechase (won by Housewarmer) and won the Valentine Steeplechase with Martin M. On the third day of the meeting both steeplechases were won by Irish horses, as were two

Caughoo exercising on the sands at Sutton, Co. Dublin prior to winning the Grand National in 1947.

of the four races run on the flat, both these latter winners being trained by Hubert Hartigan.

Sadly, the remainder of Prince Regent's career is something of an anticlimax. In attempts to fulfil Mr Rank's dream he was sent back to Aintree to run in the next two Grand Nationals. In 1947, at the age of twelve and having gone up 2lb in the weights to the crippling burden of 12st 7lb, he could only finish fourth to the surprise winner Caughoo. This race was run in atrocious conditions of rain and mist. Again Prince Regent suffered interference and made at least one bad mistake, and the ground and the weight were all against him. Even so, it was apparent to Hyde that his years and his long campaign of giving weight away all round to good horses were telling on him more and more. In the autumn of that year he showed a flash of his old fire in giving a good Aintree horse, First of the Dandies, two

years in age and 7lb in weight and beating him three lengths in the Becher Steeplechase at Liverpool. Hyde ranked this as one of his best performances, for although he once more showed his dislike of the Aintree fences and made mistake after mistake, yet when apparently beaten something inspired him on landing after the last, and he ran the younger horse out of it on the flat. In the Grand National of 1948, when carrying 12st 2lb, he was carried out by a loose horse at the fence after Becher's, but he was not really in the race at the time.

Trainer Neville Crump and owner Mr J. Proctor watch their winner, Sheila's Cottage, ridden by A. P. Thompson, cool down after winning the 1948 Grand National.

The decision was then made to bring him to England and retire him, but he showed at home so much of his old enthusiasm that Mr Rank changed his mind and allowed him to run again. Trained for him by Horris at Druid's Lodge, he won two more races, one of them at Cheltenham, where his entry into the winner's enclosure was greeted with cheers from a sporting crowd recognising the return of an old hero. He was finally retired at the age of fifteen.

The Grand National of 1947, as has been said, was won by an unconsidered outsider, Caughoo, bred in Co. Wexford by Mr Patrick Power and trained by Herbert McDowell on the sands at Sutton near Dublin. The 1948 race again fell to an Irish-bred, Sheila's

Cottage, ridden by one of the all-time Liverpool greats, Arthur Thompson from Co. Carlow. Sheila's Cottage was by Cottage out of Sheila II, a brown half-bred mare with 'a string-halt and a temper . . . who would kick you if you came close to her hind legs in the paddock'. The daughter had clearly inherited some of her dam's temperament, as her rider could testify, for he still bore the marks of her teeth in his arm when he rode her to victory.

There were many good steeplechase horses running in Ireland during these years, but space permits the mention of only a few of them. Three with more than a touch of brilliance were Revelry, Hamstar and Cool Customer. Revelry, who won the Irish Grand National in 1947, changed hands for 26 guineas as a two-year-old. Hamstar was bought for 25 guineas as a yearling; he won the Leopardstown Steeplechase and, having been passed on again for 10,000 guineas, went on to win the Irish Grand National in 1948 for Mr Blayney Hamilton. Cool Customer won seven races in a row. Another good horse, Cloncarrig, later to gain prominence in England, won the Mullingar Gold Cup in 1947 and later took the Molyneux Steeplechase at Aintree. At Galway that year Barney Nugent trained the winners of the two big races, Charles Edward in the Plate and Point d'Atout in the Hurdle. Keep Faith, who won the Galway Plate in 1946, was considered by his rider, Tim Hyde, to have a touch of Prince Regent's class about him, but he never quite lived up to that high recommendation.

3

But, of course, the most noteworthy feature of steeplechasing in those years was the emerging genius of Michael Vincent O'Brien. His first big win, oddly enough, was on the flat, to which he was to revert so successfully in later years. In 1944 his Drybob deadheated in the Irish Cambridgeshire, and Good Days, trained by him for Mr F. L. Vickerman, won the Irish Cesarewitch. A little later O'Brien, part of whose genius has lain in his ability to recognise the latent potential in future champions, was attracted by a horse called Cottage Rake who had been running on the flat but who appeared to have the makings of a high-class steeplechaser. Knowing that Mr Vickerman was looking for just such a one, he mentioned the horse to him. In the meantime Cottage Rake had been rejected as a whistler by two interested purchasers. Not to be deterred, Mr Vickerman, on O'Brien's advice, decided to take whatever chance there was with him and bought him.

In his first season in Mr Vickerman's ownership Cottage Rake won three steeplechases and followed these victories by winning the Irish Cesarewitch in 1947. In his steeplechases he was ridden

by Aubrey Brabazon, son of the successful trainer Cecil Brabazon. A polished and versatile horseman who had already won the Galway Plate three times, Brabazon was equally at home on the flat or over fences, and he was to continue to ride 'the Rake' throughout his racing career and in all his triumphs.

In the following season Cottage Rake gave O'Brien his first victory in the Cheltenham Gold Cup. After a tremendous duel with Miss Paget's Happy Home, ridden by Martin Molony, he won by one and a half lengths, his brilliant speed and acceleration from the last seeing him safely home. Happy Home was another Irish-bred, by Cottage out of Golden Emblem, a mare whom O'Brien's father, by a strange coincidence, had once owned and had sold cheaply after she had bred two fillies.

Cottage Rake was then made an automatic favourite for the 1948 Irish Grand National, but in this race he was beaten by Hamstar, to whom he was giving 3st. A light-framed horse, he never did win an Irish Grand National, the task of giving away big weights in handicaps

177

being beyond him; nor did the twisting Fairyhouse track suit his manner of racing. Later in the year O'Brien once more demonstrated his versatility by winning his third Irish Cesarewitch, this time with Hot Spring, owned by Mr Peter McCarthy, a wealthy manufacturer of mattresses and the father of a future Senior Steward of the Turf Club.

In that same year Aubrey Brabazon completed a remarkable double, for, in addition to his victory in the Cheltenham Gold Cup, he won the Irish Oaks on Masaka, trained by Hubert Hartigan for the Aga Khan. Martin Molony too was every bit as good on the flat as he was over the fences. He is generally regarded as having been as outstanding a steeplechase rider as F. B. Rees had been in his day, and he was virtually invincible in a finish. He had won the Irish Oaks in the previous year on Desert Drive, and in 1948 he defeated Morny Wing for the jockeys' championship with 89 winners, no mean achievement for a rider whose forte was over fences. Brabazon too had a great year, being second in the list with 46 winners, while Wing was third with 37.

Cottage Rake went on to win the Gold Cup in the next two years, becoming only the third horse to win it more than once. The runners-up in these two races, Cool Customer and Finnure, were both Irish bred, and both were high-class horses. In 1949 O'Brien and Brabazon brought off a notable double at Cheltenham when they won the Champion Hurdle with Hatton's Grace, a small horse by His Grace out of Hatton by Mr Jinks. Unprepossessing to look at, Hatton's Grace had originally changed hands at 18 guineas, but he beat the English crack National Spirit into fourth place that year and triumphed again in 1950 and 1951. 'In his spare time', as O'Brien's biographer has put it, he won the Irish Lincoln and the Irish Cesarewitch. It was also in 1949 that O'Brien won the National Hunt Steeplechase, the big amateur event at Cheltenham, with Castledermot, ridden by the last of the great Corinthians, Lord Mildmay of Flete.

19

Vincent O'Brien, Paddy Prendergast and Joe McGrath

1

The story of Irish racing in the 1950s is one of continued progress, the opening year of the decade being distinguished by the Aintree victory of the Irish-bred Freebooter, hailed as the best Grand National winner since Golden Miller.

On the administrative side, the use of the photo-finish camera was extended to all courses. New meetings were sanctioned for Sligo and Wexford to replace historic tracks long since defunct. Experiments were made with a film patrol camera which proved successful, and this device was in operation on the principal tracks by the end of the decade. Course commentaries were also introduced and proved universally popular with all racegoers. By adopting these new measures to improve control of the sport and to assist and increase the enjoyment of it by the public the Irish authorities were in advance of their contemporaries in England, by whom they were later also to be introduced. Despite the beginnings of creeping inflation, admission charges were pegged at 1939 levels, and an overnight declaration of runners was introduced.

The year 1950 also saw the death of F. F. MacCabe at the age of eighty-six. Since giving up training he had turned his hand to journalism and had for some years been the proprietor of the *Irish Field.*

The rise of Vincent O'Brien in the jumping sphere was to be matched by that of P. J. Prendergast on the flat. In 1950 Prendergast won his first Irish Derby with Mr F. More O'Ferrall's Dark Warrior. Earlier that year he had also won the Irish One Thousand Guineas with Princess Trudy. A superlative handler of two-year-olds, at the beginning of his career he had seemed to concentrate on these and on sprinters, but this first classic success inaugurated an all but unbroken series of victories over all distances. Before his death at a comparatively early age in 1980 he had won eight Irish Derbys,

Paddy Prendergast (right) discussing a point with Vincent O'Brien.

five Irish One Thousand Guineas, four Irish Two Thousand Guineas, one Irish Oaks and three Irish St Legers. He was champion Irish trainer in 1950, a feat he was to repeat six more times. In 1963 he headed the English trainers' list, becoming the first Irishman ever to do so. Possibly the great disappointment of his life was that he never trained the winner of the Epsom Derby, for almost every other race of importance fell at one time or another to runners sent out by him.

The next year, 1951, was one of repeated triumphs for Irish horses. Four of the five English classics fell to horses bred in Ireland. Belle of All, by Nasrullah out of Village Beauty, took the One Thousand Guineas, Ki Ming, by Ballyogan out of Ulster Lily, the Two Thousand Guineas, and Neasham Belle, by Nearco out of Phase, the Oaks. Their breeders were respectively Lord Adare, Mr J. C. Sullivan and Major L. B. Holliday, who owned the Cleaboy Stud in Co. Westmeath. A flyer from Paddy Prendergast's stable,

Joseph McGrath (left) with the Hon. W. E. Wylie at the Curragh.

Windy City, topped the two-year-old Free Handicap in England and Ireland. But best of all, of course, was the victory of Mr Joe McGrath's Arctic Prince in the Epsom Derby. Bred by McGrath himself at Brownstown (by Prince Chevalier out of Arctic Sun), trained by W. Stephenson and ridden by C. Spares, Arctic Prince trounced his field by six lengths with his rider looking over his shoulder for danger. Mr F. W. Dennis's Signal Box, another Irish colt, took third place. Signal Box had already won the Irish Two Thousand Guineas and was ridden in both these races by Martin Molony.

This was the first Irish-owned winner at Epsom since Boss Croker's victory with Orby, although the winner was not trained in Ireland as Orby had been. After the race Joe McGrath was received by royalty, an honour not conferred on his predecessor. In every respect it was Mr McGrath's crowning and well-deserved achievement both as an owner and breeder.

The next year saw Paddy Prendergast establishing another record by winning £31,731 5s in stakes, much of it for his principal owner, Mr A. L. Hawkins, for whom he won the Irish Derby with Thirteen of Diamonds and the Irish Oaks with Five Spots. Mr Hawkins's £18,963 15s in stakes won put him on top of the list of winning owners in Ireland and established yet another record, beating that of the Aga Khan, who had won £14,725 in 1948.

Tulyar, the brilliant winner of the Derby, the St Leger, the Eclipse and the King George VI and Queen Elizabeth Stakes, was bred by the Aga Khan and Aly Khan on their stud farm at Gilltown Stud in Co. Kildare.

The wedding of Vincent O'Brien and Jacqueline Witternoom on 29 December 1951. Martin Molony gives the toast.

2

In steeplechasing Vincent O'Brien continued on his winning way, taking in 1952 the Irish Grand National and the Galway Plate with Alberoni, owned by Mr H. H. M. Stanley, a member of the Derby family. As the season progressed into 1953 O'Brien had equal successes in England in what was to be an eventful year for him. He won the Cheltenham Gold Cup with Knock Hard, ridden by Tim Molony, elder brother of Martin, who was riding entirely in England and was to head the jockeys' list there for many years. Just three weeks later O'Brien won the Aintree Grand National with Early

The Curragh, 1953. Premonition and Harry Carr being led in after the Irish Derby, in which they were first past the post. 'Twenty minutes later we were disqualified' was the rider's comment on this photograph.

Mist, who had fallen at the first fence in the previous year when carrying Mr J. V. Rank's colours.

In the interval Mr Rank had died, and, his horses coming up for auction, Early Mist was bought by Mr J. H. Griffin, a rising Dublin businessman. It was an irony of fate that Early Mist should have succeeded in winning the great race for a newcomer at his first attempt where so many good horses had tried and failed for Mr Rank. Joe Griffin, or 'Mincemeat Joe' as he was called after his principal product, in his short career on the Turf must have been one of the luckiest owners in history, for he won the Grand National again in the following year with Royal Tan, also trained by O'Brien. Both these winners were ridden for him by Bryan Marshall, a brilliant Irish jockey who completed the domination of Irish riders on the steeplechasing scene at that time.

After triumphing in the Grand National with Early Mist, O'Brien turned once more to the flat. He won the Irish Derby with Chamier, albeit as a result of a controversial objection against Premonition, trained by Captain Harold Boyd-Rochfort, who was first past the post. The stewards, Major Dermot McCalmont, Sir Cecil Stafford-

184

King-Harman and Judge Wylie, all very experienced racing men, disqualified Premonition and awarded the race to Chamier. 'The Captain' made certain outspoken remarks on this decision, as did Premonition's rider, W. H. Carr, later on in his memoirs. Rickaby, the rider of Chamier, in *his* memoirs, naturally enough, took the opposite view. Nevertheless, Sir Cecil Stafford-King-Harman, who occupied the stewards' stand across the course with the Stewards' Secretary Dan Bulger (the very same position, incidentally, which Major Victor McCalmont was to occupy in an even more controversial enquiry nearly thirty years later), had and still has no doubt that justice was done. Crossing the course with Dan Bulger after the finish, he said to him: 'If there is not an objection, we shall have to hold an enquiry,' and he was not surprised, even though it was a classic race, when the objection followed. After the matter had been adjudicated upon Major McCalmont turned to him and said: 'The last time there was a successful objection in a classic was in England, and all the stewards who sat on it were dead within the year!'

Happily, in this instance precedent was not followed and, although Major Dermot McCalmont and Judge Wylie have gone to join the great senior steward in the sky, Sir Cecil is still very much with us as an active octogenarian, the doyen of the Turf Club, its senior member and an active and vastly experienced adviser at its councils.

As a result of the objection — the first in the history of Ireland's premier classic — the records show that in 1952 O'Brien trained the winners of the Cheltenham Gold Cup, the Aintree Grand National and the Irish Derby — a unique achievement.

Sensation, however, was destined to pursue O'Brien. In 1954, only a month after Royal Tan had secured his trainer's second successive Grand National victory, the Irish National Hunt Stewards sat to consider the running of certain of his horses and, following their enquiry, withdrew his licence to train for three months from 2 April of that year. O'Brien vigorously protested that the decision was unwarranted and unjust; he issued a statement to the press in which he declared: 'I am completely in the dark as to what, if any, offence I am alleged to have been guilty.'

Six months earlier the English Stewards had held an enquiry into the running of Blue Sail in the Cornwallis Stakes at Ascot. Blue Sail was trained by P. J. Prendergast and owned by the same J. H. Griffin who owned Early Mist and Royal Tan. As a result of their enquiry, the English Stewards decreed that no horses trained by P. J. Prendergast should be allowed to run under their rules and that no entries should be accepted from him. The Irish Stewards then felt impelled to hold their own enquiry, which they did on 23 October. Having done so, they stated they were satisfied with the running of Blue Sail in Ireland and that they had decided to take no further action. This decision made racing history, for it was the first time that a ruling of the Jockey Club pertaining to a horse trained in Ireland had not been followed by the Turf Club.

Neither of these reverses in any way affected the careers of the two great trainers. Far from it, for O'Brien soon went on to establish yet another record. In March 1955 Quare Times, trained by him, won the Aintree Grand National, thus making him the only trainer ever to send out three consecutive Grand National winners.

Quare Times was ridden for him by Pat Taaffe, a highly talented horseman and yet another of that brilliant generation of Irish steeplechase jockeys. Taaffe was retained by Tom Dreaper but had been released to ride Quare Times since the Greenogue stable did not have a runner in the race. Taaffe had topped the combined flat and

Lord Bicester, a great supporter of Irish steeple-chasing.

steeplechasing jockeys' list in 1953; furthermore, in that year he had had the experience of introducing to racing for Mr Dreaper a horse of Lord Bicester's who looked likely to rival if not surpass the giants of the past.

Royal Approach was just such a horse as Lord Bicester, a lifelong supporter of steeplechasing, liked to own and Tom Dreaper to train — a big, quality, rangy gelding with an eager eye. Taaffe said of him that he took his fences 'like claps of thunder', and whatever it is that makes star quality in a horse, he had it. In 1954 he won the Cathcart

187

Cup at Cheltenham, virtually running away. Back in Ireland, he was still qualified for the Maiden Steeplechase at Fairyhouse, but so brilliant was he that the decision was made to take on the older and more experienced horses in the Irish Grand National. The decision was amply justified by the result, for he put on a display of fast brilliant jumping such as had seldom been seen on the track, squandered his field, and won going away. This was his sixth successive victory, and as he went to his summer rest unbeaten that year Tom Dreaper began to think he might have another Prince Regent on his hands.

But Lord Bicester, despite his knowledge, his enthusiasm and the money he lavished on the big, bold steeplechasers he liked to see carrying his colours, was, like J. V. Rank, never a really lucky owner and, again like J. V. Rank, he never fulfilled his ambition to win an Aintree Grand National. Indeed only one Cheltenham Gold Cup fell to him, in 1951 when Silver Fame, who owed much to the matchless finishing strength of Martin Molony, got home by a short head from Mr Rank's Greenogue. Lord Bicester did not care for critics of his horses, many of whom he bought himself or in consultation with his trainer. Taaffe tells how Jack Anthony, who had retired from the saddle and taken up training, came to him after Royal Approach had won the Cathcart Cup and, in the course of congratulating him, said: 'But he's not much to look at, is he?' Lord Bicester took this almost as a personal affront, and he reacted with some warmth. 'When did you last look in a mirror?' he said.

As had so often happened before, Lord Bicester's luck did not hold with Royal Approach, for the career of this potentially great horse was tragically terminated. At grass that summer he was kicked by one of his companions, and a bone in his knee was broken. Despite rest and the best veterinary attention, though he ran once or twice more, he was never a force thereafter in steeplechasing.

3

In 1955 Joe McGrath won yet another Irish Derby with his good, if thereafter unlucky, colt Panaslipper. This victory must have been particularly gratifying for him, since Panaslipper was trained by his son Séamus on the gallops at Glencairn from which F. F. MacCabe had sent out Orby to win at Epsom. Panaslipper had in fact been second at Epsom and was thought to have been unlucky to lose in that his rider may have made too much use of him too soon. If that was the case, full amends were made at the Curragh, where he beat another unlucky colt, Hugh Lupus, decisively by two lengths. Hugh Lupus, trained on the Curragh by J. Lenihan, had won the Irish Two Thousand Guineas and had been much fancied to win at Epsom,

but a bruised foot had prevented him running. This injury and the hard ground prevailing at the Curragh immediately before the Derby had hindered his trainer putting into him the work he wanted before he contested the Curragh classic. He disappointed again when sent to run at Ascot in the King George VI and Queen Elizabeth Stakes. It was found that he was not a good traveller, and in the following year, having been kept in England, he re-established himself.

If 1956 was comparatively quiet in Irish racing 1957 amply made up for it. The flat that year belonged exclusively to Vincent O'Brien and Joe McGrath. For the classics O'Brien produced Mr John McShain's Ballymoss, bred in Meath by Mr Richard Ball, by Mossborough out of Indian Call. After being beaten in his first outing, the Madrid Free Handicap at the Curragh in April, Ballymoss won the Trigo Stakes at the Leopardstown May Meeting, defeating Joe McGrath's Chevastrid by a neck. He was then sent to Epsom for the Derby. Here he was unlucky to come up against one of the best colts of the decade, Crepello, trained by Noel Murless, who beat him by one and a half lengths in the fastest time since Mahmoud had established the record in 1936. Ballymoss then went on to win the Irish Derby at his ease and followed this up by a victory in the St Leger at Doncaster.

Mr McShain, an American millionaire, also owned Court's Appeal, with whom O'Brien won the Irish Cambridgeshire, adding yet another big handicap on the flat to his winning list.

189

The successes of Joe McGrath's horses astounded even their owner. He won the Irish Oaks with Silken Glider, an Airborne filly. Silken Glider, like Ballymoss in the Derby, was unlucky in coming up against another exceptional filly in the Epsom Oaks, for she was opposed by the Queen's Carozza, who just held on to beat her by a head. No other classic fell to the McGrath colours in 1957, though Ballyprecious was second in the Irish Two Thousand Guineas and Chevastrid won and St James's Palace Stakes at Ascot. But the list of his winners in other races would fill pages. Suffice it to say that his Roistrar, Ballynilty, Sun Invasion, Edopatic and Windsor Tonic were all successful in good handicaps; Cloonroughan won the Naas Autumn Cup, while in the Royal Whip at the Curragh in October horses owned by McGrath filled the first three places. Amongst his winning two-year-olds were Precious Hoard, Vestogan, Ballyrullah, Game Ball, Arcticeelagh and Frozen Over. At the end of the season not only did he top the owners' list, but he was also leading breeder, with his Brownstown Stud handsomely defeating

Parade for the Ulster Derby at the Maze racecourse.

190

Richard Ball, the runner-up. Séamus McGrath was leading trainer by a large margin; his total was £21,688 in stakes won as against the £15,571 credited to the man who took second place — none other than Vincent O'Brien.

4

In comparison with these achievements on the flat in 1957, the jumping side for once had relatively little to show. The Aintree Grand National was, however, again won by an Irish-bred, Sundew, by Sun King out of Parsonstown Gem, bred by Mr J. McArdle in Co. Meath. Tom Dreaper produced a likely-looking novice in Mr A. Craigie's Fortria, who won three races off the reel, and Vincent O'Brien, demonstrating his versatility once again, another one in Saffron Tartan, who won the Maiden at Fairyhouse so convincingly that many were hailing him as the winner of the next Gold Cup.

Neither of these horses quite achieved the heights foretold for them. Fortria was second in the 1962 Gold Cup after a tremendous duel with Mandarin and won a Two Mile Champion Steeplechase at Cheltenham, together with an Irish Grand National. His best distance was, however, probably just short of three miles. Pat Taaffe said of him that he never knew a braver horse, and it was his heart alone that kept him going over the longer distances. Saffron Tartan's failure to live up to his early promise was largely due to illness and a succession of training setbacks, though much later, when he had left Ireland, he did just hold on under the inspired driving of Fred Winter to beat Pas Seul in the 1961 Gold Cup.

20

1958—Annus Mirabilis

1

Further triumphs accrued to Irish horses in 1958, the greatest being that of Hard Ridden's win in the Epsom Derby. Trained by J. M. Rogers on the Curragh, Hard Ridden became the first Irish-trained horse since Orby to win the Derby. He started at the long price of 20 to 1 chiefly because, owing to his breeding, it was thought by many experts that he would not stay the Derby distance in a true-run race. He was by a sprinter, Hard Sauce, out of the French-bred mare Toute Belle II. His rider was none other than Charlie Smirke, and the story, almost certainly apochryphal, is told that after the race Smirke roundly declared: 'Hard Ridden didn't win the Derby. I did!' If this was his opinion, he certainly had some grounds for it. In an unusually slow-run race Smirke, the supreme tactician and opportunist, was allowed to dictate the pace. Seeing the horses in front of him weakening, and noticing an opening on the rails three furlongs out, he was through it in a flash and making the best of his way home before — or so it seemed — anyone else quite realised what was happening.

Hard Ridden won by no less than five lengths from Paddy's Point, another Irish-trained horse, who was ridden by G. W. Robinson, a polished and stylish jockey, who, like Brabazon and Martin Molony, was equally at home over fences and on the flat. Before he retired and turned to training he had won the Cheltenham Gold Cup on Mill House and the Grand National on Team Spirit. He finished that year as champion jockey in Ireland. A few weeks after his defeat at Epsom, Paddy's Point was again beaten into second place, this time in the Irish Derby, the victor being Sindon, ridden by the up-and-coming Liam Ward.

Kept in training as a four-year-old, Ballymoss that year raised the fame of Irish breeding and training to even greater heights than those scaled by Hard Ridden. He won the Coronation Cup, the Eclipse Stakes and the King George VI and Queen Elizabeth

Stakes and then crowned his achievements by becoming the first horse trained in Ireland to win the Prix de l'Arc de Triomphe.

But the successes of Ballymoss did not exhaust Mr McShain's and O'Brien's international successes in 1958, for the mare Gladness, who was, oddly enough, English bred, won for them the Ascot Gold Cup, the Goodwood Cup and the Ebor Handicap under 9st 7lb. The winnings thus accumulated put Mr McShain at the head of the owners' list in England, thereby making him the first American ever to attain that pinnacle.

Hard Ridden (C. Smirke) winning the 1958 Epsom Derby, the first Irish-trained winner since Orby.

2

As if these successes on the flat were insufficient for one year, 1958 also saw a horse bred, owned and trained in Ireland win the Aintree Grand National. Mr What was owned by Mr D. J. Coughlan and trained by Tom Taaffe, the father of Pat, at Rathcoole, Co. Dublin. Pat's younger brother, Thomas 'Tos' Taffe, another accomplished horseman , had previously ridden for his father but was then retained as first steeplechase jockey by Vincent O'Brien. Mr

193

Taaffe therefore engaged the strong English jockey Arthur Freeman to ride Mr What. It was once more an irony of racing that the horse of O'Brien's whom Tos Taaffe expected to ride, Sam Brownthorn, was bought by the American Mr Tim Durant to ride himself a few

days before the race. As a result, Tos was left without a mount and
had to watch another man ride his father's horse to victory.

Tom Taaffe of Rathcoole was a wonderful judge of a horse and
an immensely popular man in racing circles. It was he who had
taught his three jockey sons to ride (Willie, the eldest, rode as
an amateur), and having given them their start, he encouraged
them to their successes. Mr What was his first winner in the Grand
National. When Arthur Freeman survived a bad blunder at the
last to bring him home a winner by twenty lengths from Wynburgh
the whole Taaffe family were almost overwhelmed by the warmth
and proliferation of the congratulations they received.

Kerstin, winner of the Gold Cup and only the second mare to win
it in its history, though English owned, trained and ridden, was bred
in Ireland by Mr Cornelius Burke of Tipperary, being by Honor's
Choice out of Miss Kilcash.

3

After all these tremendous happenings, 1959 was quiet enough,
rather as if Irish racing was marking time. However, both Joe
McGrath and Vincent O'Brien continued on their winning ways,

McGrath heading the owners' list and O'Brien the trainers'. In doing so O'Brien added two more Irish classics to his ever-growing total with Mr C. M. Kline's El Toro in the Irish Two Thousand Guineas and Mr John McShain's Barclay in the St Leger. At the end of the season he announced his intention of abandoning National Hunt racing and concentrating on the flat. In steeple-chasing the Irish Grand National was won by Zonda, ridden by Pat Taaffe; his brother Tos was second on Knightsbrook, trained by his father. The Cheltenham Gold Cup fell to Lord Fingall's Roddy Owen, trained by Danny Morgan on the Curragh and ridden by Bobby Beasley, the bearer of a famous name and the grandson of Harry Beasley, whose feats in the saddle had so enriched Irish racing for so many years. At the same meeting Quita Que, trained in Ireland by Dan Moore, won the newly instituted Two Mile Champion Steeplechase.

21

Dawn of a New Era: The Blue Riband of the Irish Turf

1

If the 1950s ended quietly, the 1960s were destined to open with a sensation that rocked the racing world. Early in May 1960 the Stewards of the Turf Club, Mr Joseph McGrath, Sir Cecil Stafford-King-Harman and Major Victor McCalmont, announced that they had sat to consider Mr M. V. O'Brien's explanation of the presence of 'a drug and stimulant in the samples of saliva and sweat taken from Chamour, trained by him, after the colt had won the Ballysax Maiden Plate at the Curragh on April 20th'. Having heard the evidence presented before them, 'the Stewards withdrew Mr O'Brien's licence to train and declared him a disqualified person from May 13th 1960 until November 30th 1961'.

O'Brien immediately and indignantly repudiated any suggestion that he could be personally implicated, saying: 'I did not drug this, or any other horse, and I trust my staff. My personal gain from Chamour's victory was twenty pounds — ten per cent of the stake.'

Chamour, a son of Chamier, the winner of the controversial Derby of 1953, went on to win the Gallinule Stakes and then, when trained by A. S. 'Phonsie' O'Brien, Vincent's younger brother, came home a convincing winner of the Irish Derby. As he was being led into the winner's enclosure a storm of cheering broke out from the huge crowd, followed by a demonstration which threatened for a minute or two to get out of hand. A cheering, shouting mob, applauding the victory and shouting 'We want Vincent!', assembled in front of the Turf Club rooms and appeared to be on the point of bursting into them. Eventually the danger passed, the crowd dispersed, and peace was restored.

Throughout all this the trainer himself, far away from these scenes, preserved both his calm and his dignity. It was universally accepted that nothing became him more than his behaviour under sentence and, further, that any suggestion that he could be in any

way personally concerned could be dismissed as absurd. Very considerable sympathy was felt for him everywhere, and in December the Stewards reduced the disqualification period by six months. On his return to the racecourse he was welcomed back by Lord Donoughmore, a Steward of the Turf Club. Immediately he showed that his time in the wilderness had in no way affected his genius, for he promptly began once more to write his name into the record books. If this grave affair had any good effect at all, it was that the methods of taking samples were thereafter drastically overhauled, altered and improved.

2

In steeplechasing too another, though quieter, controversy raged. For some years now owners had been becoming more and more reluctant to risk their good horses over bank courses. The pace of steeplechasing had stepped up, and the old type of hunter-chaser who had learnt his job in the hunting field was fast disappearing. It was also becoming difficult to obtain the necessary facilities for schooling horses at speed over bank fences. These and other impediments meant that entries in point-to-points, still run mainly over banks, were falling drastically away, and even Punchestown, the very home of bank racing, was threatened. A suggestion was therefore made to construct a bush-fence course there.

The traditionalists, whom Harry Sargent would have hailed as

being of one mind with himself and the stalwarts of old, furiously resisted any attempt to tamper with the layout of the track, hallowed as it was by its long history and unique associations. Their leader was the bearded Major M. W. Beaumont, Master of the Kildare Foxhounds, which led to one of those concerned in the dispute quipping that the affair could be called a matter of 'beards versus bushes'.

The case made by the traditionalists was that the introduction of the proposed new bush-fence course and the cutting down of races over banks would mean that Punchestown would become 'just another racecourse'. The progressives' answer was that if this was not done there would in a few years be no race meeting at all. The practice of sponsoring races was becoming increasingly frequent in Ireland, and sponsors would not support races contested by small fields of indifferent horses, nor would the Racing Board underwrite substantial stakes for these races. Thus, they argued, unless change came, the meeting was in grave danger of being reduced in status to that of a second-class point-to-point.

In the event the progressives won and the meeting was saved, though it has inevitably in the change lost some of its former country, sporting and social atmosphere. In 1960 two races were run each day over the new bush-fence course, and in 1961 a hurdle race was run at Punchestown for the first time in its history. This was confined to four-year-olds and sponsored by the Cork-based firm of Mahony, being named the Martin Mahony Champion Novice Hurdle. It was won by Mrs D. St J. Gough's Gleniry.

The outstanding performance at that Punchestown meeting, however, was that of Lieutenant-Colonel W. L. Newell's Little Horse. Aged fourteen, on the first day he won the 2½ mile Prince of Wales's Stakes, and on the following day the historic Conyngham Cup over four miles carrying 11st 7lb.

In 1960 T. W. Dreaper had won the Irish Grand National with Lord Donoughmore's mare Olympia, beginning the astonishing series of seven consecutive victories in this race. And in 1961 the grey Nicolaus Silver, ridden by Bobby Beasley and bred in Tipperary by James Heffernan, won the Aintree Grand National by five lengths from Merryman II, the previous year's winner.

3

Towards the end of 1960 a project was announced which was to change the whole concept and status of Irish flat racing. It owed its inception to the drive and vision of one man — Joe McGrath. For some time he had been preparing and maturing a plan to put Ireland into the forefront of international racing. To this end he enlisted the aid and resources of the Irish Hospitals Sweepstakes. That having been done, he secured the backing of the Stewards of the Turf Club for his plan. It was then announced that, as and from the 1962 running, the Irish Derby would be sponsored by the Irish Hospitals Trust to the tune of £30,000, making it more valuable than its Epsom counterpart — indeed, the most valuable race in Europe at that time. In future the race was to be known as the Irish Sweeps Derby.

The inauguration of this great race overshadowed all other contemporary events in Irish racing, but once again there was an O'Brien triumph to herald it and to steal some of its limelight. For 1962 saw Vincent O'Brien become the third Irish trainer to send out the winner of the Epsom Derby. This was Mr Raymond Guest's Larkspur, a Never Say Die colt bred by Mr Philip Love of Marlay House Stud, Rathfarnham. Larkspur had been bought by O'Brien for Mr Guest at the Ballsbridge Sales. Knocked down at 12,000 guineas, he was the highest-priced colt ever to win the Derby at that time. He may, however, have been a lucky winner, for no less than seven of the runners, including the favourite, Hethersett, fell in a multiple collision which occurred coming down the hill to Tattenham Corner.

This victory made Larkspur an automatic favourite for the first running of the Irish Sweeps Derby. An immense crowd which included racing personalities and principal figures in the sport from all over Europe gathered to see the race. What they saw fulfilled all expectations and justified the promoter's dream, though sadly his own runner, Gail Star, played little part in it.

It still looked anybody's race turning into the straight. There the French colt Tambourine II went to the front. For a second or two he appeared to have the race at his mercy. Then, out of the ruck, the Irish colt Arctic Storm, trained by John Oxx, came on to challenge him. Arctic Storm had met trouble in the running, but once he saw daylight he put in a devastating run. The two colts then fought a tremendous battle to the post, which they passed neck and neck. The judge gave the verdict to Tambourine II by a short head. Larkspur was fourth. But although the favourite was beaten, the crowd had seen a race that they would not easily forget.

It was universally agreed that the organisation and the spectacle, together with the skilful handling of both traffic and crowds, had amply lived up to the promotion and publicity given to the event. It had placed Ireland firmly and fairly in the forefront of international racing, thus securing the objective of Joe McGrath's far-sighted project.

Since the Irish Sweeps Derby ushered in a whole new era, this seems an appropriate place to bring this short history to an end. The remainder of the story is still fresh in the minds of the public and has been so fully covered in books and press reports that it can be best dealt with by way of summary in the following brief epilogue.

22

Epilogue

1

The twenty years following the first running of the Irish Sweeps Derby saw immense changes in the whole spectrum of Irish racing. On the flat the Derby continued to dominate the season, becoming more and more every year a feature on the international scene. Vincent O'Brien too went from strength to strength. Pinning his faith largely on American-bred horses, he won, along with countless other classics and leading races, the Epsom Derby five times with Sir Ivor, Nijinsky, Roberto, The Minstrel and Golden Fleece. On the first four of these occasions the winner had the immeasurable advantage of having Lester Piggott in the saddle. Nijinsky and The Minstrel were two of the six horses who completed the Derby double at Epsom and the Curragh during the period, the others being Santa Claus, Grundy, Shirley Heights and Troy. Nijinsky became the first horse to capture the English Triple Crown since Bahram in 1935.

The Minstrel was owned by Mr Robert Sangster, who had joined forces with O'Brien to form one of the most powerful syndicates ever seen in international racing, their first winner being Boone's Cabin at the Curragh in 1974. Another of their many notable achievements was the successive victories of Alleged in the years 1977 and 1978 in the Prix de l'Arc de Triomphe.

But O'Brien was not the only Irishman to make his mark in international racing. Santa Claus, whose dual victories in the Epsom and Irish Derbys in 1964 have already been mentioned, was trained by J. M. Rogers at the Curragh, his Epsom victory giving this brilliant young trainer his second blue riband in six years. He was ridden at Epsom by the Australian 'Scobie' Breasley and at the Curragh by Willie Burke, the lad who did him. Rogers retired from training in 1970 to concentrate on his stud interests. In his short career as a trainer he had accomplished a feat never likely to be equalled by winning two Epsom Derbys with colts who cost in the aggregate

Nijinsky, Lester Piggott up, being led into the winner's enclosure by trainer Vincent O'Brien after winning the King George VI and Queen Elizabeth Stakes at Ascot, 25 July 1970.

under 1,500 guineas, Hard Ridden having been purchased for 280 guineas and Santa Claus for 1,200.

On the question of prices it is perhaps of interest to note that when Messrs Goff celebrated their centenary in 1966 they published a list of the record prices paid at their sales up to that date. Amongst these were: for a yearling colt 16,400 guineas, paid in 1964 by Beatrice, Countess of Granard, for Mr P. A. Love's Charlottesville Flyer out of his mare Skylarking, the dam of Larkspur; for a yearling filly 13,000 guineas in 1963; for a horse in

Seamus McGrath.

training 12,000 guineas in 1948; and for a National Hunt performer 8,100 guineas, paid in 1961 by Mr Charles Vaughan for Mrs C. L. Magnier's and Mr T. O'Brien's Albergo. These figures, then considered substantial to say the least, are made to appear all but derisory by the present 'telephone number' six-figure sums brought about by inflation and Arab money and now achieved at bloodstock sales throughout the world.

Joseph McGrath, senior, died in 1966, but his sons successfully carried on his racing interests, Séamus's crowning achievement being to win the Ascot Gold Cup and the Prix de l'Arc Triomphe with Levmoss in 1969. He also won the Irish Derby with Weaver's Hall in 1973. Séamus could also claim the credit of having apprenticed

Captain D. A. R. Baggallay.

to him Johnny Roe, who was nine times champion jockey on the flat in Ireland between 1963 and 1974 and who beat the winning jockeys' record established by Martin Quirke in 1923 by just one victory when he rode 87 winners in 1972. The record did not stand for long, for five years later Wally Swinburn, at the age of forty, rode 101 winners. Liam Ward, who held the championship in 1959 and 1961, was another outstanding jockey on the flat during this period. In the latter part of his career he was retained by Vincent O'Brien for his Irish runners, and for him he scored innumerable victories, the chief of which was on Nijinsky in the Irish Derby of 1970. It is worth noting too that during this period P. J. Prendergast topped the list of winning trainers in England from 1963 to 1965, and Vincent O'Brien occupied the same position in 1966 and 1977.

The period under review also saw an upsurge in sponsorship. The Irish Hospitals Sweepstakes continued to sponsor the Irish Derby, while Guinness took over the Irish Oaks in 1963 and in steeplechasing became generous sponsors of Punchestown. Irish Distillers commenced their sponsorship of the Irish Grand National in 1971. The Irish Hospitals Sweepstakes extended their sponsorship programme by establishing a new top-class hurdle in the Sweeps Hurdle, run at Fairyhouse in 1969 and 1970 and subsequently at Leopardstown, first as a conditions race but as a handicap since 1976. Leopardstown itself was taken over by the Racing Board, and its entire layout was redesigned. It was reopened in 1971 as the first really modern concourse for racing in Ireland.

On the administration side, Ireland saw its first truly 'stipendiary' steward when Captain D. A. R. Baggallay retired from a long and successful term as Keeper of the Match Book to become a stipendiary attending meetings with all the powers of an acting steward. His great experience and vast knowledge of racing in all its aspects (since before taking over his position in the Turf Club he had been a leading amateur rider and had trained successfully in Co. Meath) ensured sane and consistent control of meetings and were of immense benefit to racing generally. His sudden death in 1973 at the early age of fifty-four robbed Irish racing of its most gifted and experienced administrator, a loss which is still felt, for he was in the true sense of the word irreplaceable.

A further reorganisation took place in the 1970s when the number of Turf Club Stewards was extended to four. It was then decided that the Senior Steward and his deputy should, in the interests of consistency and continuity, serve for a term of three years instead of one as formerly.

Since his great wealth stemmed from mercantile and not landed interests, and since he was also the heir to a long racing tradition, no better choice than Major Victor McCalmont could have been made as the first of the 'new' Senior Stewards who was to steer racing under the altered system into the new era opening before it. His own racing successes were scarcely commensurate with those of his predecessors, but he had won the Irish Oaks with Agar's Plough in 1955 and he maintained the Ballylinch Stud in Co. Kilkenny in the tradition of giving employment and nurturing young stock which had been handed down to him. In 1974 he was elected to serve a second term.

Under Major McCalmont's guidance further changes took place. The Turf Club headquarters was moved from Merrion Square in Dublin to the Curragh, where a modern building was erected to house it. New equipment to cope with the needs of what had become a rapidly expanding industry was installed and up-to-date methods

Major Victor McCalmont.

adopted. Mr Cahir O'Sullivan, who came from outside racing, was brought in to administer these. Lord HolmPatrick, who had succeeded Captain Baggallay as Keeper of the Match Book, resigned his position and went to Kenya to run racing there and was so successful in his new post that he was asked to serve an extended term of office. A further loss to the administration was the resignation a few years later of Mr Jim Marsh, who had been a successful Stewards' Secretary for many years and who left to become senior stipendiary at Hong Kong.

2

During this era of change and adaptation on the flat the Irish National Hunt Steeplechase Committee retained and maintained its old constitution and traditions. In steeplechasing the 1960s were dominated by the legendary Arkle, trained by Tom Dreaper at Greenogue. The feats of this very great horse, arguably the greatest of them all, are too well known to require detailed description here. He won the Cheltenham Gold Cup three times, with ease on each occasion. His first victory was in 1964, when he slammed the previous year's winner, Mill House, who up till then had been hailed as the successor to Golden Miller, by a contemptuous five lengths. In the following year he extended the distance against the same horse to twenty lengths and won again as he liked in 1966.

Arkle was ridden in all his steeplechases by Pat Taaffe, and in twenty-eight starts this famous partnership only suffered defeat four times, occupying second and third place twice on these occasions. He was wonderfully well trained, handled and placed by Tom Dreaper and the devoted team who looked after him. Becoming a popular idol to the masses through the medium of television, he wore his laurels with the dignity that became a great champion.

Despite the fact that, yielding to popular clamour, the Aintree fences had in 1961 been made easier by sloping them and providing aprons to assist a horse to stand off, Arkle was never sent there to take his chance in the great race, possibly owing to a natural reluctance on the part of his connections to expose him to the risk of accident inherent in the running of a horse in the Grand National. If so, it was a tragic irony that his career was terminated by an injury sustained on a park course. At Kempton on 26 December 1967 in the King George VI Steeplechase he cracked a pedal bone. It was throught that the injury occurred at the second fence. Though suffering and in pain, his class and courage carried him through to finish runner-up to Dormant, a horse he would normally have left lengths behind. Despite all that the best veterinary attention, care and nursing could do, he did not recover and never raced again.

Arkle's feats overshadowed everything else during his wonderful career. But there were others. Mr Alan Lillingston won the Champion Hurdle on the one-eyed Winning Fair in 1963, becoming only the second amateur in its history to do so. Tom Dreaper, in addition to being responsible for Arkle's triumphs, won the Irish Grand National in the seven consecutive years from 1960 to 1966, a record unlikely ever to be beaten. The 1966 winner was Mrs T. G. Wilkinson's Flyingbolt, who at one time came close to Arkle in the handicap.

Flyingbolt appeared to have a great career before him, but unfortunately he suffered physical setbacks which interrupted and ultimately ended it.

In 1968 Colonel John Thompson's Fort Leney, out of his wonderful mare Leney Princess, gave Tom Dreaper his fifth Gold Cup and Pat Taaffe his fourth. In the Gold Cup the Irish run of successes continued into the next decade, for in 1970 Mr Raymond Guest's L'Escargot, bought for him by Tom Cooper of the BBA (Ireland), whose later association with the O'Brien/Sangster syndicate was to make him one of the leading bloodstock agents and buyers on the international scene (he was also responsible for the purchase of Team Spirit, who won the Grand National in 1964), won the Gold Cup, a feat he was to repeat in the following year. In 1972 Mr P. Doyle's Glencaraig Lady brought the championship back to Ireland again.

Tom Dreaper, sadly, died full of Turf honours and mourned by all who knew him in the year 1975, but his son Jim, to whom he had already handed over the reins, carried on the great tradition he had established and inspired. Immediately he produced a training feat his father might have envied and would certainly have applauded in

Arkle, Pat Taaffe up, leading over the water jump on his way to victory in the S.G.B. Handicap Steeplechase at Ascot, 14 December 1966.

sending out the winners of four Irish Grand Nationals in the five years from 1974 to 1978. The first of these was Colebridge, but his real triumph was to produce Brown Lad, a winner in 1975, 1976 and 1978, for the horse had had many setbacks and was by no means easy to train, and moreover his last victory was achieved at the age of twelve. These winners were all ridden by Tommy Carberry, a jockey who could ride a finish to rival anyone on the flat and whose horsemanship through a race recalled the great performances of the giants of the past. Jim Dreaper again emulated his father by winning the Gold Cup with Ten Up in 1976, and the popular and ebullient Mick O'Toole won it once more for Ireland with Davy Lad in 1977.

It is also appropriate to mention some of the winners of the Sweeps Hurdle, for such illustrious names as Persian War, Captain Christy, Comedy of Errors and Night Nurse appear on its roll of honour. The brilliant Monksfield never won this race, but he put two Champion Hurdles under his belt in the years 1978 and 1979. The much-loved Red Rum too was bred in Ireland, though owned and trained in England when he set up his record-breaking series of Grand National victories.

3

It is sad to have to close this history with a brief mention of a sensation which in the summer of 1981 rocked the Irish racing world and extended far beyond it. In the Irish Two Thousand Guineas of that year King's Lake, trained by Vincent O'Brien, and To Agori Mou, trained by Guy Harwood, were concerned in a close finish, King's Lake passing the post a neck in front. A stewards' enquiry was called to examine whether or not King's Lake had left a straight line and interfered with To Agori Mou's chances. Major Victor McCalmont, the chairman of the acting stewards, had watched the race from the stand across the course, the same position which Sir Cecil Stafford-King-Harman had occupied in the Premonition/Chamier affair many years earlier. Having heard the evidence offered and viewed the film of the race, the acting stewards changed the placings, demoting King's Lake to second place and awarding the race to To Agori Mou.

From this decision the connections of King's Lake appealed to the Senior Stewards of the Turf Club. At the hearing of the appeal Mr Denis McCarthy, the Senior Steward, felt himself unable to sit, since he had horses in training with Vincent O'Brien, as did Major J. de Burgh, who was concerned with stud affairs with Mr O'Brien. The appeal panel was thus constituted of Mr C. S. Gaisford-St Lawrence, the Deputy Senior Steward, in the chair, Lord Killanin, the remaining Senior Steward, and Mr John Byrne, who was co-opted as the third member. After a lengthy hearing the appeal stewards reversed the decision of the acting stewards and restored King's Lake as the winner.

A storm of controversy immediately erupted, into which it would be profitless to enter here. It is, however, an indication of the seriousness with which the matter was regarded that after the decision was announced Major McCalmont resigned from the Turf Club and the INHSC. 'When my authority is undermined like that there is no point in making myself available ever again to act as a steward at an Irish meeting,' he was quoted as saying, adding: 'Our disqualification of King's Lake had been an important, though unpleasant decision to make. It had also been one of the easiest during my many years as an acting steward.'

A detailed examination of the methods of holding enquiries and conducting appeals was thereupon set on foot by Mr Denis McCarthy, and Major McCalmont subsequently withdrew his resignation.

Farewell! Cathal Finnegan on the ground watches the Irish Grand National field leaving him after a fall at the first fence.

Irish racing now faces immense difficulties, many of them brought about by the current recession. The imposition of a crippling stamp duty, coupled with a fall in attendances and a possible decline in sponsorship owing to the falling off of profits of many industrial firms, all create problems. However, public interest in and support for steeplechasing has never been higher, though it may be declining on the flat as it passes more and more into the hands of the conglomerates and big-spending battalions. There is little doubt, though, that Irish racing will survive and conquer its problems as it has always done in the past. If the future can throw up heirs to the great traditions established by such administrators as the Marquis of Waterford, the Earl of Drogheda and C. J. Blake and by such horses as Harkaway, Gallinule and Windsor Slipper on the flat, and Golden Miller, Cottage Rake and Arkle over fences, then it has nothing to fear.

Select Bibliography

Apperley, Charles James ['Nimrod'], *My Life and Times*, ed. E. D. Cuming, London 1927

Barrington, Sir Jonah, *The Ireland of Sir Jonah Barrington: selections from his Personal Sketches*, ed. Hugh B. Staples, London 1968

Bird, T. H., *A Hundred Grand Nationals*, London 1937

Black, Robert, *The Jockey Club and its Founders*, London 1891

Bland, Ernest, ed., *Flat Racing since 1900*, London 1950

Blaxland, Gregory, *Golden Miller*, London 1972

Blew, W. C. A., *A History of Steeple-chasing*, London 1901

Blyth, Henry, *Old Q, the Rake of Piccadilly*, London 1967

Booth, J. B., *Pink Parade*, London 1933

The Brehon Law Tracts, HMSO, Dublin 1901

British Sports and Sportsmen, 13 vols, London [1908-]

Browne, T. H., *A History of the English Turf*, 2 vols, London 1931

Cook, Sir Theodore A., *A History of the British Turf*, 3 vols, London 1904

Cox, M. F., *Notes on the History of the Irish Horse*, Dublin 1897.

Creevy, Thomas, *The Creevy Papers*, selected by John Gore, revised ed., London 1963

Curzon, Louis Henry (pseud.), *The Blue Ribbon of the Turf*, London 1890

Darling, Sam, *Reminiscences*, London 1914

Donoghue, Stephen, *Just My Story*, London [1923]

Fitzgeorge-Parker, Tim, *Vincent O'Brien: A Long Way from Tipperary*, London 1974

Fletcher, J. S., *History of the St Leger Stakes*, London 1902

Gallaher, F. J., *Our Irish Jockeys*, Dublin 1874

Galtrey, Sidney, *Memoirs of a Racing Journalist*, London 1934

Graham, Clive, and Curling, Bill, *The Grand National: An Illustrated History*, London 1972

Herbert, Ivor, *Arkle*, London 1974

The Irish Horse (1934-)

Joyce, P. W., *A Social History of Ancient Ireland*, 2 vols, London 1903

Longrigg, Roger, *The History of Horse Racing*, London 1972

McCalmont, Sir Hugh, *Memoirs*, ed. and completed by Sir C. E. Callwell, London 1924

MacLysaght, Edward, *Irish Life in the Seventeenth Century*, Dublin 1979

Macready, Sir Nevil, *Annals of an Active Life*, 2 vols, London 1924

Mason, Finch, *Heroes and Heroines of the Grand National*, London 1911

Moorhouse, Edward, *The Romance of the Derby*, 2 vols, London 1908

Munroe, David Hoadley, *The Grand National*, London 1931

O'Hehir, Michael, *Leopardstown, Old and New*, Dublin 1971

Osborne, Joseph, *The Horse Breeder's Handbook*, London 1881

Richardson, Charles, ed., *Racing at Home and Abroad*, London 1927 (Includes Charles Richardson, 'British Steeplechasing', and F. F. MacCabe and Thomas E. Healy, 'Racing, Steeplechasing and Breeding in Ireland')

Richardson, J. M., and Mason, Finch, *Gentlemen Riders, Past and Present*, London 1909

Russell, Campbell, *Triumphs and Tragedies of the Turf*, London 1930

Russell, Fox, *In Scarlet and Silk*, London 1896

Sargent, Harry R., *Thoughts on Sport*, London 1894

Seth-Smith, Michael, *Lord Paramount of the Turf*, London 1971

Smirke, Charlie, *Finishing Post*, London 1960

Sporting Life, compilers, *The British Turf and the Men Who Have Made It*, London 1906

Suffolk, Henry Howard, Earl of, Coventry, Arthur, *et al.*, *Racing and Steeple-chasing*, The Badminton Library, London 1886

Taaffe, Pat, *My Life and Arkle's*, London 1972

Voigt, C. A., *Gentlemen Riders At Home and Abroad*, London 1925

Waterford, Henry Beresford, 3rd Marquis of, *A Hunting Journal*, privately published, Dublin 1901

Watson, S. J., *Between the Flags*, Dublin 1969

Willett, Peter, *An Introduction to the Thoroughbred*, London 1966

Williams, G. St J., and Hyland, Francis P. M., *The Irish Derby, 1886-1979*, London 1980

Willoughby de Broke, John Verney, Baron, ed., *Steeplechasing*, The Lonsdale Library, London [1954]

Winter, Sir Ormonde, *Winter's Tale*, London 1955

Index